Enhancing Accountability in Public Service Delivery Through Citizens' Charters

Published by
ACADEMIC FOUNDATION
in association with

Institute of Public Enterprise

ABOUT THE AUTHORS

R.K. Mishra, Senior Professor and Director, Institute of Public Enterprise (IPE), Hyderabad, did his PhD from University of Rajasthan. A Visiting Fellow at London Business School (UK), he also studied for International Teachers programme at SDA Bocconi, Milan. Dr Mishra taught at the University of Bradford and was a Visiting Professor at Maison Des Sciences De L' Hommes, Paris and Faculty of Economics, University of Ljubljana, Slovenia. He is a member of the UN Task Force on International Standards of Excellence in Public Administration and Education. He is special invite on OECD Working Group on Privatization and Corporate Governance of SOEs and Asian Network of Corporate Governance. He is Non-Executive Director on some of the public and private enterprise boards in India. He has considerable experience of teaching and guiding research for doctoral degree in management, economics, public administration and commerce. His areas of interest include: corporate governance, international management, international finance, public-private partnership and restructuring and environmental administration.

Geeta Potaraju, Assistant Professor at the IPE, Hyderabad, is a PhD in Management with specialisation on public sector enterprises. She has over 15 years of experience in management and development consulting. Her areas of expertise include: participatory governance and civic engagement, health system strengthening, administrative reforms, institutional reforms, change management and capacity building. She has been involved in a number of key assignments with DFID, UNDP, World Bank, World Bank Institute, Family Health International, Government of India and state governments. She is an expert on participatory governance tools like citizens' charters and community score cards, and has trained a number of officials from Government of India as well as other state governments on these tools.

Enhancing Accountability in Public Service Delivery Through Citizens' Charters

The Indian Experience

R.K. Mishra
Geeta Potaraju

ACADEMIC FOUNDATION
NEW DELHI

www.academicfoundation.org

First published in 2015
by

ACADEMIC FOUNDATION
4772-73 / 23 Bharat Ram Road, (23 Ansari Road),
Darya Ganj, New Delhi - 110 002 (India).
Phones : 23245001 / 02 / 03 / 04.
Fax : +91-11-23245005.
E-mail : books@academicfoundation.com
www.academicfoundation.com

in association with
Institute of Public Enterprise, Hyderabad.

Disclaimer:
The findings/views/opinions expressed in this book are solely those of the authors and do not necessarily reflect the views of the publisher.

Cataloging in Publication Data--DK
Courtesy: D.K. Agencies (P) Ltd. <docinfo@dkagencies.com>

Mishra, R. K., 1948- author.
Enhancing accountability in public service delivery through citizens' charters : the Indian experience / R.K. Mishra, P. Geeta.
pages cm
ISBN 9789332703094

1. Public administration--India. 2. Government accountability--India. 3. India--Charters, grants, privileges. I. Geeta, P., author. II. Institute of Public Enterprise (Hyderabad, India)issuing body. III. Title.

DDC 351.54 23

Typeset by Italics India, New Delhi.

Printed and bound by The Book Mint, New Delhi.
www.thebookmint.in

Contents

1

Evolution of Citizen's Charter

The phrase 'citizen's charter' was used for the first time by John Major, the former Prime Minister of UK, in his speech to the Conservative Central Council on 23 March 1999.[1] The focus was on systematically examining the public service delivery mechanisms and to ensure that higher standards of service delivery could be achieved by government agencies. Thus, the UK launched the citizen's charter scheme for the first time in 1991, with a purpose to improve public service delivery, to make it more responsive to the citizens, and ensure that they get their entitlements which they rightfully deserved.

> It will work for quality across the whole range of public services. It will give support to those who use services in seeking better standards. People who depend on public services—patients, passengers, parents, pupils, benefit claimants—all must know where they stand and what service they have a right to expect.
>
> John Major.

The purpose of the charter was to guarantee quality service delivery to people and provide redressal of grievances in case of non-delivery of committed services. Transparency was the key word driving the agenda, and therefore, it was decided that standards for every service should be published, both as a benchmark for improvement and to show the public what they could expect in clear terms from various government departments/ministries. As a part of the UK Citizen's Charter programme, it was also proposed that the performance reports be made accessible to the common man so that he/she could know how local services were being delivered and how they were measured. The system also created scope for providing financial incentives for

1. The birth of citizen's charter is given in the autobiography of John Major, the former Prime Minister of UK, 1999.

good performance (performance-related pay) as well as financial sanctions for service failure. One of the main features of the charter programme was to establish a robust complaints management system to ensure that citizens get their grievances redressed through a laid out procedure and are compensated adequately.

The UK Government brought out a white paper on Citizen's Charter in 1991 which indicated that the scheme was not a uniform 'blueprint' for service provision, but a 'toolkit' to allow standards to be raised in the way most appropriate to each service.[2] It meant that the charter was more of a mechanism to facilitate service improvement by a public agency. One of the key aspects of the citizen's charter initiative was the creation of individual service charters. The basic idea of the charters was that they would form a kind of contract between service users and service providers. The charters were meant to be a tool which would inform citizens of their entitlements to public services, and give a clear direction to the service providers regarding the level and standard of service delivery that they had to commit to; this created a situation where the service providers were encouraged to improve both standards and responsiveness to service users, and by the year 1997, the UK had 42 national charters covering the main public services and over 10,000 local charters.[3]

The key principles of public service on which citizen's charters were based on are:[4]

- Standards.
- Openness.
- Information.
- Choice.
- Non-discrimination.
- Accessibility.
- Grievance Redressal.

---

2. *The Citizen's Charter: Raising the Standard.* Cm 1599. Report of the House of Commons, July 1991, p.4.

3. *From Citizen's Charter to Public Service Guarantees: Entitlements to Public Services.* Report from the House of Commons Public Administration Select Committee, 2007–08, 12th Report.

4. Ibid.

Standards

Citizen's charters were meant to display explicit standards which were published and prominently displayed at the point of delivery. Standards included courtesy and helpfulness from staff and commitment to prompt action well within the declared timelines.

Openness

Citizen's charter is based on the philosophy that there should be no secrecy about how public services are run, how much they cost, who is in charge, and whether or not they are meeting their standards. Public servants should not be anonymous except in cases where there is a real threat to their safety, and all those who deal directly with the public should wear name badges and give their name on the telephone and in letters.

Information

Full and accurate information should be readily available, in plain language, about the services which are being provided by a public agency. The idea is to encourage transparency and accountability in the public service agency through the citizen's charter programme.

Choice

The public sector should provide choices wherever practicable and people affected by the services should be consulted. The views of the citizens using services should be sought regularly, and systematically to take informed decisions about what services should be provided.

Non-discrimination

Citizen's charter encourages equal treatment to all, which means that public services should be made available to the citizens regardless of their race or sex. Information on the services must also be printed in minority languages.

Accessibility

Services should be made available to the citizens in a convenient manner. The service provider must offer flexible opening hours, accommodate emergencies and provide facilities to people residing in far/remote areas.

Grievance Redressal

In case anything goes wrong and the citizens don't get the services that they are entitled to from the government agencies, then every citizen is entitled to a good explanation, or an apology. He or she should be told why the train is late, or why the doctor could not keep the appointment so on and so forth. There should be a well-publicised and readily available complaints procedure. If there is a serious problem, it should be put right. And lessons must be learnt so that mistakes are not repeated. Grievance redressal system is a key component of a citizen's charter initiative, and must incorporate all of the above stated features.

The citizen's charter initiative was assessed by the government in 1997, and the Public Service Committee in its report concluded that the initiative made valuable contribution to improving public services (Cabinet Office, 1998). The Committee found that the citizen's charter led to improvements in the delivery, culture and responsiveness of many services, the committee also acknowledged that although not all of the observed changes to public services were directly attributable to the charter's implementation, it certainly played a key role in improving service delivery. One of the main benefits of the charter programme for the supply and demand side has been that it has lessened the public deference towards the service providers and improved their readiness to accept poor services, at the same time it has also taught the service providers to accept the views of users and take them as constructive feedback for bringing about improvements in service delivery. The major criticism regarding the citizen's charters was that the charters prepared by the public service agencies were vaguely worded and the promises declared in the charters were meaningless (Cabinet Office, 1998). It was perceived that the citizen's charters were more of a declaration of intention of the government and what they proposed to achieve in terms of service delivery rather than what could actually be achieved on the ground. It is also reported that the citizen's charter lost public respect because it was seen as being too confused in its objectives.

In 1998, the Government introduced 'Service First: The New Charter Programme', with a view to effectively respond to the needs and wishes of people who use public services on a daily basis. This would give public servants the chance to show their dedication, enthusiasm and initiative, in an effort to work together to improve the communities they serve. The main idea behind the Service First programme was to provide an opportunity to all the public services delivery organisations, nationally and locally, to set out clear standards of service and report their performance. This programme was also proposed to involve the users in carrying out these tasks so that there are systems provided for redress. The principles of Service Standards for government departments were laid down clearly:[5]

- Answer your letters quickly and clearly. Each department and agency will set a target for answering letters and will publish its performance against this target.
- See you within 10 minutes of any appointment you have made at its office.
- Provide clear and straightforward information about its services and at least one number for telephone enquiries to help you or to put you in touch with someone else.
- Consult its users regularly about the services it provides and report on the results.
- Have at least one complaints procedure for the services it provides, and send you information about a procedure if you ask.
- Do everything that is reasonably possible to make its services available to everyone, including people with special needs.

Despite all the criticism that the charter programme faced from various quarters, it still remains one of the most effective citizen-centric initiatives with a clear idea to empower the users/citizens at large and bring in accountability to public service delivery. As an

5. The Public Service Committee, *Third Report of Session 1996–97*, The Citizen's Charter, HC 78–I, para 92.

extension to this programme, the Government of UK initiated a Charter Mark (CM) award which was given to agencies implementing citizen's charters and demonstrate high standards of quality in delivering.

Global Interest in Adopting Citizen's Charter Programme

The UK's Citizen's Charter generated a great amount of interest around the world and several countries implemented similar programmes. Many adopted citizen's charter model based on the UK experience: Belgium (Public Service User Charter 1993), France (Service Charter 1993), Canada (Service Standards Initiatives 1995), Australia (Service Charter, 1997), Malaysia (Clients' Charter, 1993), Spain (The Quality Observations, 1993), Portugal (The Quality Charter in Public Services), India (Citizen's Charter, 1997), Jamaica (Citizen's Charter, 1994) (Parigi and Geeta, 2002).

The Government of Malaysia issued Guidelines on the Client's Charter in 1993 to assist government agencies to prepare and implement Client's Charter, which is a written commitment by an agency to deliver outputs or services according to specified standards of quality. A Best Client's Charter Award was instituted in 1993. The Malaysian system of Client's Charter closely follows the UK Model. A distinction is made between agency-wide and unit charters. There is a concept of service recovery which mandates taking steps to restore the trust and confidence of the client in a proactive manner when things go wrong.

The Commonwealth Government of Australia launched its Service Charter initiative in 1997 for improving quality of service delivery to its citizens and making government services more accessible and simpler to use for the citizen. The government provided for a one-stop shop facility for its citizens to access government services. The Treasury Board of Canada Secretariat started a Service Standard Initiative in 1995 based on the citizen's charters model of the UK.

Adoption of Citizen's Charters in India

The governance scenario in India was fast changing in early 1990s with the introduction of liberalisation and globalisation regime. The citizens had become more articulate about their needs and expectations from the administration. People expected the government to not merely respond to their demands, but also to anticipate them and prepare for delivery well in advance. In the year 1996, a general consensus emerged in the government on the need for an effective and responsive administration to satisfy people's aspirations. In a conference of chief ministers of various states and union territories held on 24 May 1997 in New Delhi, presided over by the Prime Minister, an "Action Plan for Effective and Responsive Government" was developed which was broadly agreed by all in the political spectrum and administrative units.[6] It was decided that the central and state governments with large public interface would develop citizen's charters for services like railways, telecom, post, PDSs (public distribution systems) etc. These charters were required to include service delivery standards along with timelines for delivery, and to be presented to the general public in a user friendly manner. The Indian charters have been primarily adopted from the UK model, but they have certain additional components which cater to the Indian psyche. New elements have been added to the Indian version of the charters such as 'expectations from the clients' or in other words 'obligations of the users' have been added to the charters to make it more useful in the Indian context. Another very important element in the development of charters in India has been the involvement of consumer organisations, citizen groups, and other stakeholders in the formulation of the citizen's charter to ensure that the charter meets the needs of the citizens.

Citizen Empowerment and Citizen's Charter Implementation

In the Indian context, citizen's charter was developed on the philosophy of citizen empowerment. The citizen's charter goes a long way in making the life of the citizen easy and at the same time creates a sense of accountability on the part of the organisations to provide the promised services to its customer, thus, empowering the citizens with customer rights. A citizen's charter empowers people to know and demand right

6. *Action Plan for Responsive Administration*, evolved by the Government of India at the Chief Secretaries Conference, New Delhi, 1997.

services from the organisation. Citizen empowerment becomes possible through the flow of information from the organisation to the citizens. Figure 1.1 explains this cycle of empowerment.

Figure 1.1

Citizen Empowerment Cycle

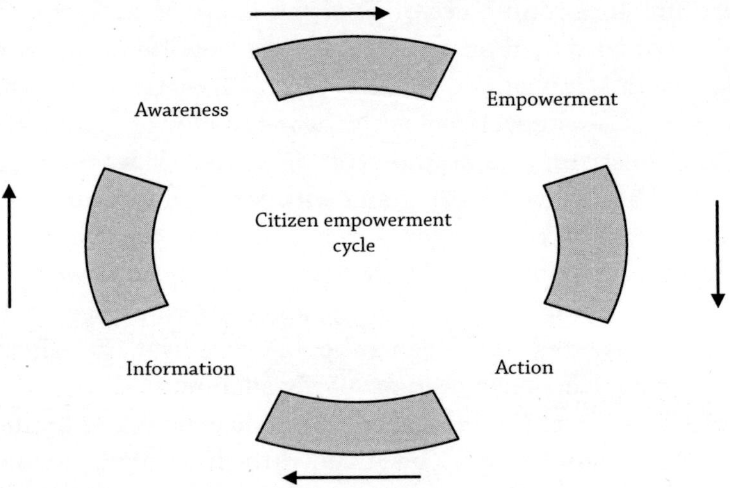

The empowerment cycle involves three important interrelated components, i.e., information flow, awareness creation and resultant empowerment.

Concept of Citizen's Charter: The Indian Version

A citizen's charter is the expression of an understanding between the citizen and the public service providers about the quantity and quality of services citizens receive in exchange for their taxes. Fundamentally, it envisages both the rights of the public and the obligations of the public servants. As public services are funded by citizens, either directly or indirectly, through taxes they have the right to expect a particular quality of service that is responsive to their needs and is provided efficiently at a reasonable cost. The citizen's charter is a written and voluntary declaration by service providers about their service standards, choice, accessibility, non-discrimination, transparency and accountability in accordance with the expectation of the citizens (Parigi and Geeta, 2002).

Citizen's charter is a tool which facilitates a change in the mindset of the public official from someone with power over the public to someone who is responsible to provide them with necessary services. The Government made all the possible efforts to ensure that citizen's charter should not simply remain a document of assurances, but function as a tool kit of initiatives and ideas to raise the level of standards of service delivery. It was meant to become an effective tool to ensure transparency and accountability and facilitate delivery of good governance by various departments. The Indian charter was modelled on the lines of British charters. The various components included in the citizen's charter were as follows (Parigi and Geeta, 2002).

- Published standards for service delivery.
- Openness and information about service delivery.
- Choice for the citizen and consultation with users about service levels and quality.
- Courtesy and helpfulness in service delivery.
- Provision of redress when services are not delivered to the published standards.

Published Standards

The citizen's charter lays out explicit standards of service to be delivered by various departments/ministries and enforces accountability by publishing the standards of service delivery, so that users understand what they can reasonably expect for each service. The citizen's charter is a tool relevant both to the users and the service providers. There is a tendency on the part of the department/ministry to select areas for setting standards based on their own convenience and purely internal point of view of the organisation. Citizen's charter provides an opportunity to change the attitude of service providers and to develop service standards that are measurable, meaningful, realistic, challenging and monitored periodically. Departments were advised to refrain from including standards which are heavily loaded with intent, but are not measurable. For example, if a transport department says that: "We will ensure that 90 per cent of the buses will reach destination in time", is of no use because the customer is more interested in knowing the standard relating to punctuality, how frequently the buses will ply and in which routes etc. Furthermore, agencies have been discouraged from using vague statements and promises such as 'it will be our constant endeavour,' 'we will try our utmost,' and 'it is our objective' while developing standards; standards should be measurable and specific.

Information and Openness

Citizen's charter promotes transparency, and the key attribute of good service is that it should provide concise information to the users at the right time and at the right place. The public agencies have to develop citizen's charters with full and accurate information, written in simple language about the services to be expected from the agency, at what standards the services will be delivered and details of the person who is in charge of service delivery. Charters must also highlight the process in case the services are not delivered as per the declared standards. Publication of hand books, guides, posters and providing information on websites are some of the ways of providing information.

Choice and Consultation

The citizen's charter formulation process must necessarily involve the users of various services. There should be regular and systematic consultation with the users of the service through formal and informal channels and their views about services and their priorities for improving them should be taken into account in finalising standards.

One of the important features of the Indian charters is the idea of balancing the citizen's rights with his responsibilities. This should reflect in the process of development of the charter, and the citizens' involvement and cooperation must be sought in realising these objectives set out in the charters. For example, the charter might set out that a given service can be provided within a certain time frame, but only if the citizen cooperates with the officials concerned, for example, by providing the right information for a driving licence application, etc.

Courtesy and Helpfulness

The citizen's charter initiative helps in embedding a culture of courteous and helpful service from public servants. Citizens expect that departments must provide services equally to all who are entitled, suiting their convenience. May I Help You counters, and Information and Facilitation Desks should be available at all offices to help citizens understand the procedures and what is expected of them. In particular, these should cater to the disadvantaged groups and minorities.

Courtesy is evidenced by:	*Good service is evidenced by:*
Welcoming citizens visiting the government offices.	Doing what is needed.
Receiving citizens with a smile.	Assisting and giving advise.
Apologising for delayed attention and saying sorry if you are unable to help.	Providing information and solving problems.
Expressing thanks.	

Grievance Redressal: An Integral Part of Charter Implementation

Developing an effective grievance redressal system is an integral component of the citizen's charter programme in India. Each public authority is expected to set up a robust grievance redressal mechanism with appropriate procedures for addressing citizen complaints in their respective units. Service providers should welcome complaints as a means of getting feedback in order to improve services. If things go wrong, an apology or a full explanation followed by a swift remedy should be offered. Redressal systems should be: quick, accurate, consistent, inexpensive, simple and individually focussed.

Proactive Role of Government of India and Charter Implementation

Government of India (GoI) has taken a very proactive role in promoting the concept of citizen's charter and also assisted various central and state governments in capacity building for effective formulation and implementation of charters. Initially at the national level, the Department of Administrative Reforms and Public Grievances (DARPG) was the nodal agency which initiated the task of coordinating, formulating and operationalising citizen's charters. Guidelines for formulating the charters as well as a list of dos and don'ts were communicated to various government departments/organisations to enable them to bring out focussed and effective charters. For the formulation of the charters, the government agencies at the centre and state levels were advised to constitute a task force with representation from users, senior management and the cutting-edge staff. A comprehensive website of citizen's charters in GoI (*www.qoicharters.nic.in*) was developed and launched by the DARPG on 31 May 2002. This website provided information on the citizen's charters issued by various central government ministries/departments/organisations. With the objective of generating awareness among the citizens as well as government functionaries of the commitments of various organisations enshrined in their citizen's charter, the DARPG brought out a Compendium of abridged versions of all citizen's charters in GoI containing details of various services provided by each department with their published delivery standards and quality of services proposed to be provided along with the public grievance redress mechanism as committed in the citizen's charters.[7] The Compendium contained the name, address, telephone number, e-mail address, etc., of nodal officers for citizen's charters in central government ministries/departments/organisations and also the list of website addresses of ministry/department/organisation concerned. The Compendium proved to be a very useful ready reference for the citizens and also enabled them to critically review the functioning of these organisations.

In order to spread awareness on formulation and implementation of charters in various states in India, regional seminars and workshops on citizen's charters were organised by the GoI. The initial workshops were conducted by the Centre for Good Governance, Hyderabad, which

7. Website of the Performance Management Division, Cabinet Secretariat, New Delhi, *www.performance.gov.in*

was the agency responsible for capacity building on citizen's charter supporting the DARPG. The purpose of the workshops was to bring national and state level organisations along with other stakeholders including NGOs (non-government organisations), intelligentsia, media, etc., on the same platform to share knowledge and experiences in formulation and implementation of citizen's charter (Parigi and Geeta, 2002).

In order to effectively establish performance culture, the GoI established a Performance Management Division (PMD) in the Cabinet Secretariat in January 2009. The key mandate of the PMD is to establish mechanisms for performance monitoring and performance evaluation in government departments on a regular basis. It involves preparation of a Results Framework Document (RFD) by each department every year. The RFD highlights the departmental objectives and priorities for the current financial year as well as the achievements of the department against those pre-specified targets indicated in the RFD at the end of the year. Thus, RFD works as an accountability tool and provides the government departments focus to deliver effectively and efficiently. It helps in bringing about objectivity to the working of government departments and facilitates measurement of performance of the government agencies so as to make necessary improvements wherever required. RFD as a tool also provides an opportunity to the agencies to demonstrate, to the citizens at large, the efforts being taken up by them to improve their service delivery and in the bargain enhance their credibility and improve citizen perception on government services. As on March 2013, 200 citizen's charters have been formulated by the central government ministries/departments/organisations and 629 charters by various agencies of state governments and administrations of union territories (Parigi and Geeta, 2004). Most of the national charters have been posted on the government's websites and are available for viewing to the public. The service delivery organisations which have developed citizen's charters also take necessary initiatives to give publicity to their charters through print/electronic media and awareness campaigns.

Annexeure A-1.1

Charters of Select Departments

Dos and Don'ts for Implementing the Charters

S.No.	*Dos*	*Don'ts*
1	Make haste, slowly.	Don't merely make haste.
2	List areas of interface.	Don't be unrealistic.
3	Phase out areas for introduction of small steps.	Don't take on more than you can commit.
4	Involve customer and staff in formulating and implementing it.	Don't involve only senior officers in the formulation and implementation.
5	Prepare a Master Plan for formulation and implementation over five years and budget for it.	Don't rush into an overall package for the whole Ministry/Department/ Organisation.
6	Win consumer confidence with small, highly visible measures.	Don't promise more than you can deliver.
7	Remember citizen's charter is a process, constantly evolving.	Don't look upon it as a one-time exercise, with a final outcome.
8	Inform the customer of the proposed commitments.	Don't inform the customer unless you are sure of delivering the service.
9	Use simple language.	Don't use difficult language or jargon.
10	Train your staff.	Don't leave yourself out.
11	Delegate powers.	Don't centralise.
12	Set up systems for feedback and independent scrutiny.	Don't continue blindly without regular periodic reassessment of performance.

Annexure A-1.2

Flowchart on the Main Features of Developing the Charter

Decentralisation of administrative and financial powers is the key for successful charter implementation.

The following flowchart gives a comprehensive map for developing a charter from the different stages such as planning to drafting, consultation to launch, distribution to monitoring.

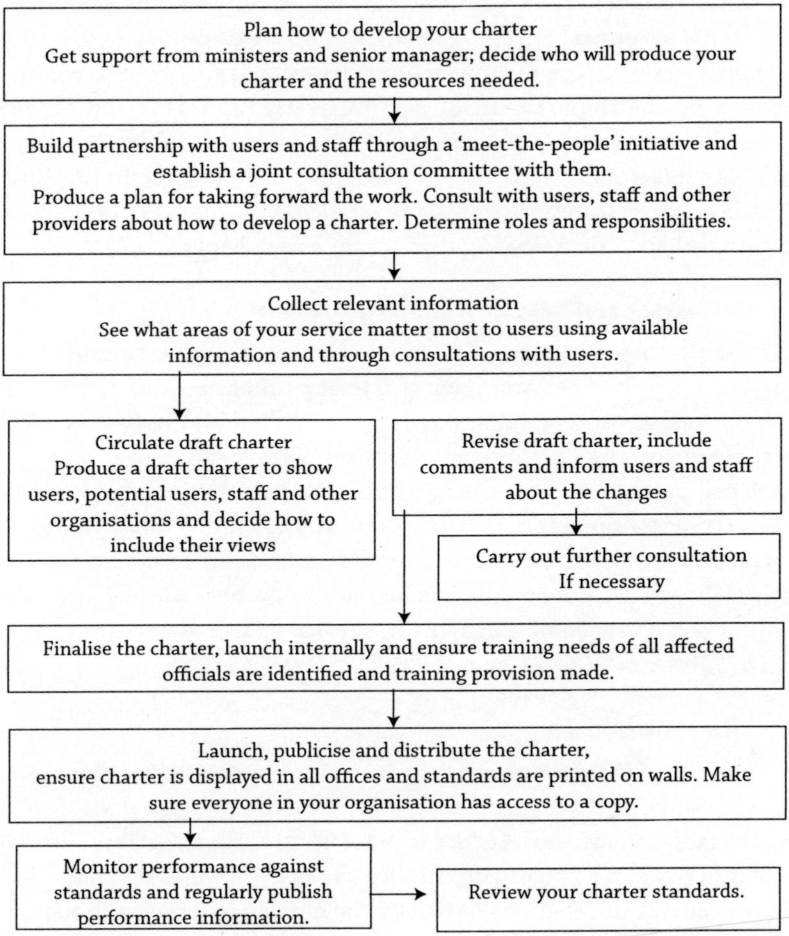

Annexure A-1.3

Redefining Service Delivery Excellence in India: Sevottam

With the change in political scenario after 2004, the GoI refocussed on the citizen's charter programme. The Second Administrative Reforms Commission (ARC) was constituted by the GoI, Ministry of Personnel, on 5 August 2005. The purpose of its constitution was to prepare a plan of action for a complete makeover of the public administrative system. The Second ARC in its 12th report entitled, "Citizen Centric Administration: The Heart of Governance" recommended that the administration must be made transparent, accountable and citizen friendly. The report recommended Sevottam model for making administration citizen centric, which was developed by the Department of Administrative Reforms and termed as 'Sevottam' which means *uttam seva* or excellence in service delivery.[8] Sevottam model was developed with the overarching objective of improving the quality of public service delivery in the public service delivery organisations. Sevottam includes the following three main components.

Citizen's Charter and Service Standards

Citizen's charter is an initiative wherein the department/ministry declares its key services along with delivery timelines and requirements. Sevottam focuses on the formulation, monitoring and review of citizen's charter to ensure the organization promises what it can deliver and delivers what it has promised. Even though citizen's charters were being prepared by departments/agencies, it was felt that they were done without the involvement of citizens/clients/stakeholders and there was no relation to service delivery improvement. Inadequate awareness among the citizens regarding the presence of a charter in service delivery agencies is another concern. Sevottam is designed to fill the lacunae.

Public Grievances

Sevottam focuses on receipt, redressal and prevention of grievances. Although some of the central and state government agencies developed grievance redressal system, it is not in place in many organisations. Even if the system is in place in some organisations, grievances are not taken as feedback for improvement of services. Especially the employees are not inducted into

8. Guidelines on Citizen's Charters released by the PMD, Cabinet Secretariat, Government of India, New Delhi, 2013.

this system and are not oriented towards the grievance redressal mechanism. Sevottam is designed to establish the culture of grievance redressal.

Service Delivery Enablers

Sevottam is the third pillar as enabler of service delivery such as customer feedback, employee motivation and infrastructure. Most of the times, the government agencies don't have a proper infrastructure facility to deliver the service. Aspects of customer feedback and employee motivation are not very familiar terms in most government organisations. Personnel are not involved in planning and implementation and are generally de-motivated due to lack of training and capacity building at the cutting-edge level.

The Sevottam Model

The Sevottam model consists of a number of criteria to ascertain how well the organisation is tuned into the requirements of the three components elaborated above. However, before the organisation undertakes a systematic assessment, it needs to have some basics in place. The basic eligibility conditions as well as the next level of criteria are explained in the following subsections. The first component of the model requires effective charter implementation thereby opening up a channel for receiving citizens' inputs to determine the way in which organisations determine service delivery requirements. Citizen's charters publicly declare the information on citizens' entitlements, making citizens better informed and hence empowering them to demand better services. The second component of the model, 'Public Grievance Redress,' requires a good grievance redress system operating in a manner that leaves the citizen more satisfied with how the organisation responds to complaints/grievances, irrespective of the final decision. The third component, 'Excellence in Service Delivery,' postulates that an organisation can have an excellent performance in service delivery only if it manages the key ingredients for good service delivery well, and building its own capacity to continuously improve delivery.

A very good example of Sevottam compliance is the Central Board of Excise & Customs (CBEC)—an IS 15700 certified organisation. Sevottam scheme was launched in the year 2007 to standardise service delivery to the taxpayers. CBEC identified the services delivered to different taxpayer segments and promised definite time lines for delivery of these services. The first citizen friendly single window Aayakar Seva Kendra (ASK) to roll out these services was set up at Pune. Today 15 ASK centres are functional in the country. CBEC has adopted Centralised Public Grievance Redress and Monitoring System (CPGRAMS) at all-India level as a robust grievance redress system. It has developed delivery capability at field offices to meet IS 15700 stringent norms and designed a Service Quality Manual on how to deliver quality in taxpayer services as per the industry best practices. The aim is to provide taxpayer in terms of timeliness in delivery, single window facility, trade facilitation and proactive feedback collection.

Assessment Model Application

Modules (3)	*Criteria (9)*
	1.1 Implementation
Citizen's Charter	1.2 Monitoring
	1.3 Review
	2.1 Receipt
Public Grievance Redress	2.2 Redress
	2.3 Prevention
	3.1 Customers
Service Delivery Capability	3.2 Employees
	3.3 Infrastructure

References

Cabinet Office (1998). *Service First: The New Charter Programme*. June p.1.

Parigi, V.K. and P. Geeta (2002). *A Guide to Developing and Implementing Citizen's Charter.* Centre for Good Governance, Government of Andhra Pradesh.

———. (2004). *Proceedings of the Regional Capacity Building Workshops.* Conducted for the Department of Administrative Reforms & Public Grievances. New Delhi.

2

Citizen's Charter: Toolkit

A citizen's charter is the expression of an understanding between the citizen and the public service provider about the quantity and quality of services citizens receive in exchange for their taxes (Parigi and Geeta, 2002). As public services are funded by citizens, either directly or indirectly through taxes, they have the right to expect a particular quality of service that is acceptable to them and is provided at a reasonable cost. The citizen's charter is a written, voluntary declaration by service providers about service standards, choice, accessibility, non-discrimination, transparency and accountability. Therefore, it is a useful way of defining for the customers, the nature of service provision and explicit standards of service delivery.

The citizen's charter document by the department/organisation indicates the following aspects of service delivery such as:

- What services will be delivered?
- To whom will the services be delivered?
- When will it be delivered and mode of delivery?
- Where and how of service delivery?
- Who is responsible for the delivery?
- Of what level of quality will the service delivery be?

The chapter provides a detailed step by step guide for formulation and implementation of citizen's charters (Potarajn and Parigi, 2006).

For any department to formulate a citizen's charter, there are a few steps that need to be kept in mind. These are indicated as follows.

Step 1: Preparatory Groundwork

The preparatory groundwork for formulation and development of citizen's charter basically includes some activities which an organisation must undertake. Firstly, there must be clarity in the organisation as to why it is developing a charter and what it proposes to achieve through the implementation of the charter. A policy decision needs to be taken on the issue of implementation of the charter.

Some of the steps involved in the preparatory stage include:

Setting up of a Core Group

Formation of a core group is essential in the organisation consisting of representatives from all stakeholders who, *inter alia*, may include members from the top to middle management and cutting-edge level, staff representatives, strategic partners, and customers/clients. This group will essentially undertake the responsibility of preparation and implementation of the charter.

Analyse the Need for a Charter

Primarily an organisation must analyse the reasons for why it needs a charter. This will help the organisation to gain clarity on how it would want to go about the implementation of the charter. Another issue that needs to be addressed is how will the implementation of the charter affect the functioning of the organisation. Will it help the organisation to perform better, streamline service delivery, etc.? These are some basic questions that need to be addressed by an organisation before developing the charter.

Revisiting the Objectives

Identifying the Vision and Mission of the organisation is important in context of citizen's charters. The objectives to be achieved through the implementation of the charters must be clear. Every organisation must look at the activities they are performing and focus on how the development of a charter will enhance the scope of reaching their organisational goals and purpose.

Explanation: In order to deliver services efficiently you need to understand several aspects such as, Why your department exists? What is its role? What is your role as a departmental functionary? Are you doing it well? How can we perform better? Answering these questions will help:

Mission and Vision of Your Department	*What Services Does Your Department Offer to Citizens?*	*What are the Key Functions Performed?*	*What are the Key Processes Followed? Are the Processes Transparent?*	*Is There Scope for Improvement?*

Identifying External Stakeholders

The most important issue to be addressed while making a citizen's charter is identifying the external stakeholders of the organisation and taking them into confidence. This will bring in a sense of ownership among various stakeholders, which is critical for the effective implementation of a charter. The stakeholder group will include all of the following: users, the citizen representatives of the users, citizen advocacy groups, consumer organisations, parents (in the case of schools), politicians, past and potential users, and others.

Sample Questions You May Pose!

1. How many users/citizens/customers does the agency meet everyday? Tick the appropriate box.

   1-10 ☐

   11-20 ☐

   21-30 ☐

   31-50 ☐

   51-75 ☐

   75-100 ☐

   Above 100 ☐

2. Who are these users of the services your department offers? (e.g., general public, students, farmers, women, children, the aged, industries, contractors, etc.) Please list them out.

   1.

   2.

   3.

   4.

   5.

3. What percentage of the above meets you for the following purposes?

   For information ___%

   For approvals/applications, certificates ___%

   Other purposes (please specify) ___%

   Are these needs being met by some other department also? Yes/No

   Is there a duplication of services? Yes/No

   If your answer is yes, please mention the names of the departments duplicating the service.

4. Prioritise the needs of your users.

S.No.	*User Type 1*	*User Type 2*	*User Type 3*	*User Type 4*
1.				
2.				
3.				
4.				
5.				

Identifying the Internal Staff to be Involved in the Charter Initiative

The public agency must focus on how to involve staff and take into account their views on what the charter should cover. Identification of a core group to work on the charter is an issue to be addressed while formulating the charter. Positively inducting the employees and employee representatives—who are involved in delivering the standards set out into the citizen's charter programme—will go a long way.

Identification of Suppliers

Suppliers involved in providing parts of the service, e.g., the engineers involved in providing service must also be identified and involved in the process of charter formulation and implementation.

Establishing Institutional Arrangements for Implementation

Infrastructure and governance arrangements are required to be put in place in the process of implementation. There is a need to assess the implications on resource for developing a charter—in terms of time and money (including to what extent can we afford to pay compensation to citizens in case of failure to deliver and how will we provide it). These issues have to be clearly identified.

Checklist proposed: Are you ready for citizen friendly governance? What are your department's efforts in this area?

Environment in the office		
Have you installed a citizen's information desk?	Yes ☐	No ☐
Do you have 'May I help you' counters?	Yes ☐	No ☐
Are the persons manning these desks friendly, responsive and efficient?	Yes ☐	No ☐
1.1.1 *Courtesy and helpfulness*		
Are you treating citizens with courtesy?	Yes ☐	No ☐
Are you being helpful and quick with your responses/services?	Yes ☐	No ☐
Accessibility		
Are the concerned officials available to citizens in the hours earmarked for public interviews?	Yes ☐	No ☐
Do you have multiple channels (phone, Internet, literature) for citizens to obtain routine information without visiting the office?	Yes ☐	No ☐
Feedback		
Is there a feedback/complaint box in your office?	Yes ☐	No ☐
Is there a feedback system to measure citizens' satisfaction with your services?	Yes ☐	No ☐
Willingness to listen and act		
Do you have a citizen advisory committee that gives consultations or feedback on policies, service delivery, etc.?	Yes ☐	No ☐

Attitudinal Changes

Establishing contact and engaging with your customers/ stakeholders is one of the most crucial steps towards citizen friendly governance. Customers must be made aware of the charter and its significance. For designing and implementing citizen's charter in a department, there are certain prerequisites that need to be built into the system. For instance, the department must encourage a culture of openness and welcome feedback, criticism and citizen interaction.

Step 2: Identifying the Service Delivery Parameters and Service Standards

Identification of Key Services

One of the most important aspects of developing a citizen's charter is to select the services delivery criteria to be offered to the users. It is also very important for the department or the agency to define appropriate standards for service delivery which must be agreeable for all the stakeholders including internal staff who are supposed to deliver the services.

For example, please list the services delivered by your department to various users?

		Target Audience/User		
S.No.	*Category of Service*	*User Type 1*	*User Type 2*	*User Type 3*
1				
2				
3				
4				
5				

Identify Service Standards in a Consultative Manner

Providing services to citizens in a timely and effective manner is crucial for effective implementation of the citizen's charters. Therefore, it is necessary that the organisations clarify their service delivery timelines and ensure that they are being implemented. Developing service standards in a realistic manner is the most important activity in charter formulation.

The following actions are critical during this phase:

- Listing out the various services being delivered by the department/agency to different users.
- Identifying the time taken for delivering the service. In this particular activity, you must necessarily involve the operational units/planning units of the organisation so that the services are aligned well with the service standards published in the charter.
- This activity must be done in consultation with citizens, otherwise the standards set may not relate to aspects of service that citizens prioritise, or they may be set either too low or too high.
- It is also important that the service standards must be time bound, realistic, achievable, measurable and specific. If not, the citizen will become cynical about the charter. For example, the standards should not say that officers will 'do their utmost,' a statement that is neither specific nor measurable.

Suggested Format

S.No.	*Category of Service*	*Times Lines for Service Delivery*	*Required Documentation*	*Nodal Point*
1				
2				
3				
4				
5				

While developing the service delivery standards it is also important to keep in mind the quality aspects. Some parameters for defining quality service include:

- Reliability: consistency in performance.
- Responsiveness: timely service, grievance redressal, complaint management.
- Credibility: having citizens' interests at heart.

- Courtesy and helpfulness: how citizens are received in government offices, how they are treated, spoken to, etc.
- Enthusiasm: physical willingness to serve.

Taking Feedback on the Service Standards from Stakeholders

It is extremely essential to take feedback on what is a good service, which includes service standards, quality, timeliness, etc. It includes process efficiency, friendliness to employees as well as other unforeseen factors. This needs to be done in consultation with stakeholders. Without it the charter is just a statement of intent rather than a live, meaningful—if voluntary—contract between the state and the citizen. This is a time-consuming and costly exercise and should be carefully planned. A stakeholder is someone who has a stake or interest—direct or indirect—in the service being delivered, that is anyone who benefits from or has a direct interest in the service. The various sub-activities under this stage include:

Preparation of a Stakeholder Engagement Plan

Once the stakeholders are identified, the next step is to institutionalise links with them and bring them into the organisational fold. If there is a Nodal Officer in the organisation in charge of the charter, that person should be responsible for devising a 'stakeholder engagement plan'.

Some guidelines for formulating a citizen engagement plan:

- Meet with them at least twice during the period of developing the charter, firstly to ask their views on what should be included, and secondly to show them the charter that has been developed as a result of their views.
- Engage them periodically thereafter, especially at the time of review of the charter, which should take place annually.
- Ensure that a meeting is organised with them during or soon after the busiest period of your work, so that they are commenting on the service at its most stretched.
- Keep the agenda open so that citizens feel they have been consulted and listened to.

Step 3: Essential Features of a Citizen's Charter

A citizen's charter is a document representing the organisation's systematic efforts to focus on its commitments towards its citizens with respect to standards of service, information, choice and consultation, non-discrimination, accessibility, grievance redress, courtesy, and value for money. It also includes the organisation's expectations from the citizens for fulfilling its commitment.

Formulating Citizen's Charter

As per the guidelines provided by the Performance Management division for developing citizen's charter for a ministry/department, the following nine sections are key components for developing a citizen's charter:[1]

- Cover page.
- Vision.
- Mission.
- Service Standards.
- Grievance Redress Mechanism.
- Stakeholders/Clients.
- Responsibility Centre.
- Indicative expectations from service recipients.
- Month and Year for next review of the charter.

Preparation of a citizen's charter involves identifying the services, deciding the timelines, looking at the compensation, etc. There are some essential issues that need to be kept in mind while drafting a charter.

Here are some tips that must be kept in mind while drafting a charter:

- Keep the Charter Short and Punchy: The citizen's charter must be essentially short, punchy and must convey clearly the details of the organisation, its activities, its purpose, and the standards set by the organisations to reach the standards.

1. Website of the Performance Management Division, Cabinet Secretariat, New Delhi. *www.performance.gov.in*

- Use Simple Language and Avoid Jargon: The citizen's charter must be prepared in a very simple language. No jargons must be used in the charter or it will defeat the objective of the charter.
- Use of Local Language: The citizen's charter must essentially be brought out in the local language, apart from the official language of the region.
- Clarity in Presentation of Charter: The citizen's charter must be presented in a simple manner which can be understood by all citizens and the charter must be able to fulfil the objective with which it was conceived.
- Make the Charter Attractive But Not Glossy: Although the charter must be simple and clear, yet it is essential that it is presented in an attractive manner to the users.

Improving your Processes

Improving service delivery means focusing on the processes. Especially in a public agency which is meant to deliver services to general public, there must be clear cut processes, which are faster, simpler and easier to complete. Only then will the citizens reap the benefit of government subsidies and programmes. What are processes in a public agency: making payments or submitting applications are both processes. How can these be improved? You could:

- Check if the present process is right.
- How much time does a citizen take to submit the application or make payment?
- How many counters does he have to visit to complete the job?
- Does he go back from the office contended that his job is done?
- If no, then is there a need to redesign the process/create a new process?
- Reduce red tape.
- Reduce waiting time.
- Reduce paperwork.
- Use IT (information technology) to improve the process.
- Outsource.

Process improvement follows naturally when you ask and tackle these questions:

1. Where are the delays?
2. Where is the duplication?
3. Where is the bottleneck?
4. Where are the unnecessary checks?
5. Is there unnecessary movement of people, records and files?
6. Can we remove/reduce intermediate steps?
7. Can we open green channels or a single window service?

Develop Appropriate Formats and Designs

Developing of formats and designs is an essential activity in the formulation of citizen's charters. The format and design of the charter will influence the attitude of the public to the charter initiative, as it will probably establish their first impression of it. The presentation of the charter should make people want to use it and make it easy for them to do so. The guidelines developed by the Performance Management Division (PMD) on Citizen's Charters' implementation have provided essential formats which the department may use during the process.

Design Compensation Package

If the citizen's charters implementation has to be effective, it is essential to compensate citizens in case of non-delivery as per the established norms. This may lead to compensation from the organisation or from the individual responsible for the lapse. This has been a weak link in the Indian scenario, the state governments have experimented with the scheme of penalising officials for not delivering the service as committed, but has not been very successful.

Step 4: Design and Develop Information and Facilitation Counter

After the preparation of the charter is completed, it is essential to put in place an information desk which will facilitate in the dissemination of information.

Establishing May I Help You Counters

Setting up of counters to assist public will provide fillip to the implementation of the charters. Setting up Citizen Information Centres or the Citizen Information Counters manned efficiently will promote the citizen's charter implementation and will bring in greater awareness in public. The biggest problem that people usually have with government offices is the number of people they need to meet to get a simple job done. Even something as common as obtaining approval for a building plan, requires the document to pass through the hands of more than 50 government officials. Most people feel very lost in a government office and often, several days go by before they are directed to the right person. In such a context, what is needed is an Information Facilitation Centre (IFC).

- The centre must be as near the entrance as possible and prominently sign-boarded.
- IFC to provide information on services, schemes and procedures concerning the department.
- IFC to provide all required forms used for various procedures.
- Provide brochures, booklets and reports that will give more information.
- The centre to be manned by competent employees who will personally, or over the phone, direct users to the correct officers or guide them on procedures and documentation required.
- The IFC to receive complaints and also issue acknowledgement slips indicating the section dealing with the subject.
- The IFC must provide all forms and materials required by subscribers and act as a single window help desk.

Activity Proposed:

1. What steps would you take to set up an IFC in your department?

    a.

    b.

    c.

2. What are the stages to starting an IFC in your office?

   Stage 1

   Stage 2

   Stage 3

   Stage 4

   Who are the individuals or groups primarily responsible for this task?

   1.
   2.
   3.
   4.
   5.

   When (date/month/year) will this work be accomplished?

   1.
   2.
   3.
   4.
   5.

Generating Awareness on Charters

Creating awareness is very important for effective implementation of the charters. Therefore a sound publicity strategy has to be designed in order to make the charter a success. Using print and electronic to spread the message will go a long way in creating awareness about the charters. Citizen's charters need to be advertised. This does not necessarily mean big spending—it just means that every single person in your office and every single person who walks into your office must be aware and made aware that there is change in the air. The charter must be prominently displayed. Attention must be drawn to it with the assurance that every word in meant. Citizens must be made aware that they can expect a certain quality of service from you.

Initiating a Dialogue

Creating awareness by initiating a dialogue with citizens about their needs and expectations from public services is critical to the success of the charter. Regular dialogues with citizens' advocacy groups (such as user groups) and directly with citizens will be effective in creating awareness and also at low costs, as these groups have their own internal communication networks. Other ways of generating awareness include simple approaches like ensuring that the copies of the charter are widely available, are distributed at helpdesks and in offices with a public interface. Similarly, displaying the charter's standards on the walls in government offices will leave no citizen in any doubt about the charter's existence.

A formal review of awareness creation should be undertaken through occasional surveys about the charter. This should lead to a review of strategies used to raise awareness about the charters and selection of the same according to the needs profile of the users.

Some of these strategies are:

- Visuals, films, TV, street plays, posters;
- Field-to-field, open house meetings, face-to-face discussions;
- Audio messages, radio, public announcements;
- Touch screen kiosks, websites.

Winning Citizens' Confidence

It is necessary to gain confidence from the citizens' on the effectiveness of the charters and they need to be convinced that it is an effective tool for improving service delivery.

Launching Direct Helplines

Helplines could be established through which citizens can gather necessary information on citizen's charters.

Handbooks and Guides on Services

Publishing of user guides and handbooks will provide the necessary information that citizens need. It will help in setting a right direction and in assisting the public on the use of charter.

Establishing One-stop Shops

One-stop shops could be set up where citizens can complete all their transactions in one place.

Calling up and Writing Customers Telephonically to Assess their Needs

Proactively calling the citizens' telephonically and writing to them and enquiring about their needs will also create a positive environment and will create trust in the minds of the people.

Inviting Customers to the Office and Familiarising its Activities

Inviting customers to the office and briefing them about the activities of the organisation is also a method to involve the citizens in the process.

Activity: What is the Status of these Actions in Your Department?

S.No.	*Action points*	*Done*	*To be done*	*When will it be done?*
1.	Displaying the charter in a prominent place in your office			
2.	Does every member of your office have a copy of the charter?			
3.	Does your department have a website?			
4.	Are copies of the charter freely available?			
5.	Have you established call centres?			
6.	Do you have an email response system?			

Step 5: Establishing a Grievance Redressal Mechanism

Grievances handling is an essential in-built mechanism in the process of citizen's charter implementation. It is necessary that the organisations have in place a robust grievance redressal mechanism (GRM) so that complaints from citizens can be handled effectively. An effective GRM system is a prerequisite for the effective functioning of citizen's charters.

There is a strong link between the provision of good quality service and dealing well with grievances. This relationship is based on two main elements. Firstly, by facilitating and responding to grievances, the cause for the grievance can be rectified. Any organisation that aims to provide good quality service must understand clearly when and where it is failing. There are a couple of things that the organsiaiton can do to make this happen:

Acknowledge Complaints

a) Personalise responses;
b) Talk to customers if possible;
c) Send letters.

Designate a Location in the Office to Receive Complaints and Make it Accessible and Visible to Customers

A separate space must be allotted to the complaint management cell where the person incharge will receive, acknowledge and answer queries on the status of complaints.

Develop a System for Record-keeping

Keeping record of the complaint is essential, this helps the organisation to identify the areas for improvement.

Process, Record, Investigate and Analyse Complaints

The complaints must be recorded, acknowledged and redressed. These are the essentials of an effective complaints management system. The information generated by the grievances helps it to put matters right for the user/citizen. Secondly, identifying the 'trends' in grievance helps the organisation to resolve systemic and recurring problems for the benefit of all its users.

Keep the Customer Informed of the Progress

The citizen must be kept informed about the status of his/her complaint so that he is aware of the fact that his problem is being addressed.

Analyse Complaints Periodically

In order to identify the needs of the customers, regular analysis of the complaints must be taken up. Evaluation and monitoring of the grievances received is also a vital component of the charter initiative. All inquiries should be recorded in an appropriate manner. Systematic classification of grievances received by the organisation should be done which will help to identify and rectify systemic or recurring problems. Classification should be done regularly clearly giving the nature of complaint, complaint's name, location and date, responsible officer, referrals, nature of action taken when and by whom, if action not taken why. This kind of data helps the senior management to take corrective action and find where shortfalls are occurring.

Feedback from Staff and Public

One of the most important prerequisites for getting feedback is to make it easy for the citizen to provide it. This includes, among other things, ensuring that officials who are accountable are available to meet the citizens at the times specified.

The different methods for getting feedback could include:

- Over the Counter at Service Outlets.
- By Toll Free Telephone Number.
- Through Regular Post, e-mail, Fax and Telephone.
- *Via* Community and Consumer Organisations.
- Consultative Committees.
- Periodic Written Surveys.

Other methods include:

A suggestion box: The most direct way of getting feedback, of course, is at the point of contact. Every citizen must have the opportunity to tell you what he/she thinks and a suggestion box is the simplest way. Make sure there is writing material near the box.

A small questionnaire: A brief questionnaire asking the citizen to fill out asking what they came in for, whether their visit was fruitful and how long it took for their needs to be catered to, etc. This would go a long way in assessing how your 'front-office' staff is doing for customer-friendliness.

Follow-up: A follow-up telephone call to make sure that the customer is happy with services or products creates a lot of good will for your department. E-seva followed up service with a survey and found that their service actually yielded desired results.

Mailed questionnaires: These are useful for slightly long-term feedback, to see how you've performed over three or six months.

Customer contact: Senior officers must interact often with customers to assess what their needs are and if your department is meeting them to satisfaction. Tata Telecom, for example, asked their senior managers to sit in the service counters and interact with customers. As a result, the feedback they got proved invaluable.

Customer surveys: A survey—either a formal one through an external agency, or one conducted by your own department staff—can tell you much about what your customers think of your services, what else they need and avenues in which you can improve.

Focus groups: Meeting consumer organisations also reveals much about expectations from your department. LIC recently held meetings with consumer organisations to sound out issues of policy holders and realised that there was a need to introduce new products and services.

Multiple channels of communication: The citizen must be able to contact your department through various channels—through telephone, post, e-mail, fax, the Internet and in person. All numbers and addresses must be well publicised, so your customer has no trouble reaching you.

Activity: What is Your Action Plan as Far as Collecting Feedback is Concerned?

	What is the Current Position?	*When will you Start to Implement it?*	*What Improvements do you Expect after Implementing it?*
Setting up a suggestion box			
Small questionnaire at the point of contact			
Mailed questionnaire			
Focus groups			
Customer surveys			

Step 6: Evaluation and Monitoring

It is very important that departments carry out an evaluation of citizen's charters implemented on a regular basis. Evaluation can be taken up in many ways such as exit polls for user groups, surveys and feedback could be used. It is very important that evaluation should take place regularly, ideally quarterly. Offices which have proper IT infrastructure must go in for IT-based assessment process so that data can be analysed in real-time and reports generated automatically on service failure against the charter standards. It is also advised that these evaluations must be carried out by a third party.

It is also important that self-assessment should be practised with staff to assess how well they think they are delivering services. This can be compared against feedback from customers. Feedback can be taken up in any one ways including:

Reviews with Staff

The staff involved in the charter implementation could consolidate their observations and impressions on the process of implementation. This makes a valuable feedback document for the organisation for further strengthening.

Internal Surveys using Feedback Systems

Internal survey can also throw light on how the charters are being implemented.

Face-to-face Meets with Users Visiting the Office

Feedback from the visitors could give substantial proof on how the charter is being implemented.

External Reviews

External reviews are very essential to study the impact of charter programme. These evaluations could be conducted through voluntary organisations, research organisations, consumer activists, universities, colleges, consultants, or any other methods could be used. The PMD has initiated an independent audit of the department's Citizens'/ Clients' Charters (CCC) which is a mandatory indicator as a part of the Results Framework Documents (RFDs) developed by all the central government departments.[2] The departments/agencies are required to submit a self-assessment report on their implementation of citizen's charter. Apart from this report, there are parameters identified for assessing a department on the implementation of its citizen's charter as indicated below.

Degree of Visibility of the Charter

In order to assess the degree of visibility of the charter, the following indicators are used:

- Is the charter of the department displayed in the reception or facilitation centre?
- Is the charter displayed on the home page (main menu) of the department's webpage?
- Is the charter displayed at grievance redress office?
- Is the charter displayed in the office of the nodal officers?
- Is the copy of the charter made available to the audit team at the reception desk or help desk?

Awareness of Departmental Officers/Staff about the Charter

In this particular category, an attempt is made to see whether the officer designated to implement the citizen's charter is aligned well to his role and upholds the standards set in the charter:

- To ensure timely delivery of service or transaction within a prescribed time.
- To increase accountability of service provider.
- Effective redressal of grievances in case of non-compliance by service provider.
- Display of charters at prominent places such as the facilitation centre/reception desk/website.
- Orientation/training of concerned officials/staff of the department is essential to improve the effectiveness of charter implementation.

2. Ibid.

Transparency and Availability of Information

The citizen's charters are meant to be tools for enhancing transparency and accountability of a government agency. A charter details out the services provided by the agency along with information on the timelines and standards of service delivery. During the evaluation of the charter, it is mandatory to see if the charter has the contact numbers of the officials responsible for service delivery along with their names and contact numbers as well. The charter practically must provide all the information that a citizen is looking for about a particular agency.

Responsiveness

As a part of the citizen's charter programme, there is a built in mechanism of setting up a grievance redressal system by the department. It is basic essential element of citizen's charter programme. Reducing the waiting time for service delivery-response rate for the phone calls made to contact persons is one of the key indicators for assessing an agency on effectiveness of charter implementation. During the audit period, random calls are made to officers providing services and grievance redress officers on different working days, and at different points of time within the working hours, to see if the call is picked and the concerned person is available to speak.

At the end of the year, each department submits a self-assessment report containing details of departmental performance *vis-à-vis* targets on the charters to the PMD. The report contains all details of service/transaction with a short description, who provides it, how is it measured, where do the data come from, mitigating strategies adopted to prevent data manipulation, how frequently measurement is done, etc.

The Detailed Evaluation Methodology is provided in the Annexure A-2.1.

Conclusion

There are a number of lessons that an organisation/department would learn and a number of deficiencies would be noticed during the course of implementation of citizen's charter. Identifying the problems and avoiding the mistakes will go a long way in stabilising the system and in providing beneficial results. As the charters raise the aspirations of the users of the service, the departments should guard against the tendency to promise more than they can deliver. A realistic assessment of the capabilities of the service provider must be taken into account in drafting the charter. A commitment to specific services standards should be made only if they really can be delivered. A critical review of the current systems and processes in the department should be undertaken to examine whether they are likely to have an adverse impact on the charter. Failure to do this will result in a mismatch between the standards enumerated in the charter and the capacity of the system to deliver. Implementing the charters without the staff owning them will defeat the purpose of the charter. Motivating the staff and involving them in the preparation of the charter are important. The charters will remain merely a paper exercise of limited value if there is no consultation with the users. Departments should ensure citizen involvement at all stages of preparation and implementation of the charter.

Independent audit of results is important after a period of implementation of the charter. The charter is meant for the users and departments may not know how they are faring unless their performance is tested against the standards. Unnecessarily complex systems for lodging complaints, access to officers, obtaining redressal of grievances, defeats the purpose and the spirit of the charter.

References

Parigi, V.K. and P. Geeta (2002). "A Guide to Developing and Implementing Citizen's Charter", Centre for Good Governance, Government of Andhra Pradesh.

Potarajn, Geeta and V.K. Parigi (2006). *A Guide to Developing and Implementing Citizen's Charters for Local Self Government Institutions in Kerala.* Prepared for the Modernising Governance Programme (MGP), Government of Kerala. Centre for Good Governance (CGG), Hyderabad, February 2006.

Annexure A-2.1

Evaluation Methodology for Citizen Charter

The Performance Management Division (PMD), Cabinet Secretariat, initiated an independent audit of the department's Citizens'/Clients' Charters (CCC). As we know that the implementation of charters have been unsatisfactory and therefore the government decided to include "Development of Citizens'/Clients' Charters" in Results Framework Documents (RFDs) as a mandatory indicator for all Departments. The RFDs have the following mandatory indicator:

Actions	*Success*	*Unit*	*Weight*	*Target/Criteria Value*				
				Excellent 100%	*Very Good 90%*	*Good 80%*	*Fair 70%*	*Poor 60%*
Independent Audit of implementation of Citizens'/ Clients' Charter (CCC)	% of implementation	%	2	100	95	90	85	80

The independent audit was based on the following criteria.

	Success Indicator	*Unit*	*Weight*	*Target/Criteria Value*				
				Excellent 100%	*Very Good 90%*	*Good 80%*	*Fair 70%*	*Poor 60%*
A.	Degree of visibility of CCC in relevant area	%	10	100	85	75	60	50
B.	Awareness of departmental officers/staff about CCC	%	10	100	85	75	60	50
C.	Degree of accuracy of the numbers and names of the contact person in CCC	%	10	100	85	75	60	50
D.	Response rate for the phone calls made to contact persons	%	10	100	85	75	60	50
E.	Quality of the self-assessment report	%	10	100	85	75	60	50
F.	CCC Score as calculated by the department	%	50	100	85	75	60	50

Methodology for Evaluating Each of the Six Success Indicators:

A. Degree of visibility of CCC in relevant area:

The degree of visibility of CCC will be verified by the audit team by physically visiting the respective Ministry/Department, concerned official and their website to check the following five indicators.

	1	*2*	*3*	*4*	*5*	*5= 3x4*
	Success Indicator	*Unit*	*Weight*	*Yes*	*No*	*Weighted score*
i.	Is the CCC of the Department displayed in the Reception or Facilitation Centre?	%	20			
ii.	Is the CCC displayed on the Home Page (Main Menu) of the Department's webpage?	%	20			
iii.	Is the CCC displayed at Grievance Redress Office?	%	20			
iv.	Is the CCC displayed in the office of the CCC Nodal Officers?	%	10			
v.	Audit team was able to get a hard copy of CCC at the Reception Desk or help desk	%	30			
			Total Weighted Score =			

The score awarded for this indicator is determined as follows

Total Weighted Score (from above) (from above)	5	4	3	2	1
Score Awarded for this criterion	100	90	80	70	60

B. Awareness of departmental officers/staff about CCC:

Based on Interviews with nodal officer and two officers-in charge of any service/transaction, the information is gathered for each of the following five questions relating to the purpose of the CCCs.

i. Goal of CCC is to ensure timely delivery of service or transaction within a prescribed time
ii. Goal of CCC is to increase accountability of service provider
iii. Service Recipient can avail remedies in case of non-compliance by service provider

iv. CCC should be displayed at prominent places such as the facilitation centre/reception desk/website

v. Orientation/training of concerned officials/staff of the Department is essential to improve the effectiveness of CCCs.

Each concerned officer is asked by the audit team whether he/she believes in the above are TRUE or FALSE. The rating scale for this criterion will be as follows:

Number of 'TRUE' answers	5	4	3	2	1
Score Awarded for this criterion	100	90	80	70	60

C. Degree of accuracy of the numbers and names of the contact person in CCC:

Degree of accuracy is checked by randomly calling on the contact number listed in CCC for the person responsible for a given service/transaction in CCC. This is done for 2 such officials and one grievance redress officer. The scoring based on following metrics:

	1	2	3	4		5
	Success Indicator	*Unit*	*Weight*	*Yes*	*No*	*Weighted score*
i.	Is the contact number of the person responsible for service/transaction # 1 accurate?	%	20			
ii.	Is the name of the person responsible for service/transaction # 1 accurate?	%	20			
iii.	Is the contact number of the person responsible for service/transaction # 2 accurate?	%	20			
iv.	Is the name of the person responsible for service/transaction # 2 accurate?	%	20			
v.	Is the contact number as well as name of person responsible for grievance redress accurate?	%	20			
				Total Weighted Score =		

The score awarded for this indicator determined as follows

Total Weighted Score (from above)	*5*	*4*	*3*	*2*	*1*
Score Awarded for this criterion	100	90	80	70	60

D. Response rate for the phone calls made to contact persons:

During the audit period, five calls will be made to officers providing services and grievance redress officers on different working days and at different points of time within the working hours to see if the call is picked and the concerned person is available to speak. During each attempt, if successful in contacting the concerned person, a score of '1' will be given or else '0' will be assigned. The rating scale for this criterion will be as follows:

Number of 'CALLS' answered	*5*	*4*	*3*	*2*	*1*
Score Awarded for this criterion	100	90	80	70	60

E. Quality of the self-assessment report:

At the end of the year, each department will submit a report containing self-assessment of departmental performance *vis-à-vis* targets in their CCC to PMD containing details like:

1. Details of service/transaction with a short description.
2. Who provides it?
3. How is it measured?
4. Where does the data come from? What mitigating strategies have been undertaken to prevent data manipulation? That is, what is the quality assurance procedure with respect to data?
5. Who measures it?
6. When is it measured? That is, how frequently it is measured?

The PMD recommends that the audit be taken up by a reputable Third-Party.

3

Legal Framework for Public Service Delivery in India

Efficiency in public service delivery is critical in the Indian context because most of these services are used by economically weaker sections and there are large numbers of people who are using these services in this country. These services are delivered by central government, state governments, as well as local administration. These basic services include health, education, sanitation, welfare, justice among others. These services are usually accessed by the general public as they are affordable and mostly free of cost or made available at a very low cost.

After 64 years of Independence, Government of India (GoI) in the past few decades implemented a number of pro-citizen legislations which are meant primarily to empower citizen of this country. Some of the key initiatives include the Right to Information (RTI) Act (2005) which confers on the citizen's right to access government information including its activities, while the National Rural Employment Guarantee Act (NREGA) confers rights to citizens, guaranteeing 100 days of employment for every rural family in India. Another key initiative is the Right to Education Act which guarantees education to all children from 6 to 14 years of age, while the proposed National Food Security Act focuses on providing food security to families of low income groups. The Public Service Guarantee Acts, also known as Right to Service Acts, have been passed by many states in India. These initiatives have gained strength from the declaration of the Supreme Court of India on its declaration of right to food, health, housing, as well as several other social and economic rights to citizens.

Many state governments have enacted the Right to Public Service Acts based on their experiences of the citizen's charter initiatives in the late

1990s and early 2000s. Citizen's charters were implemented under the directions of GoI and therefore the commitment from the organisation was not very high. However, during the implementation, it was felt that these charters lacked the precision necessary to be effective. Evaluation studies have been conducted by government from time to time.

An evaluation of the citizen's charters of various government agencies was carried out by the Department of Administrative Reforms and Public Grievances (DARPG), GoI and Consumer Coordination Council, New Delhi, an NGO (non-governmental organisation), in October 1998. This was done at the nascent stage of implementation and the results were quite encouraging and no major challenges were observed (Parigi and Geeta, 2002).

In 2002-03, DARPG engaged a professional agency to develop a standardised model for internal and external evaluation of citizen's charters in a more effective, quantifiable and objective manner. This agency also carried out evaluation of implementation of charters in 5 central government organisations and 15 departments/organisations of Andhra Pradesh, Maharashtra and Uttar Pradesh (UP). This agency was also required to suggest methods for increasing awareness, both within the organisation and among the citizens, and to suggest possible methods for orientation of management and the staff in the task of formulating and deploying charters (Parigi and Geeta, 2002).

As per the report of evaluation carried out by the agency, major findings were:

- In majority of cases charters were not formulated through a consultative process.
- By and large service providers were not familiar with the philosophy, goals and main features of the charter.
- Adequate publicity to the charters was not given in any of the departments evaluated. In most departments, the charters were only in the early stages of implementation.
- No funds were specifically earmarked for awareness generation of citizen's charter or for orientation of staff on various components of the charter.

Later in 2007, a detailed evaluation was done by Public Affairs Centre, Bangalore, which highlighted certain interesting findings on charter implementation (Public Affairs Centre, 2007). The study tracks the progress and effectiveness of this reform and assessed nearly 760 charters from across the country, followed by interviews with more than 1,100 end-users and over 320 officials from diverse departments. The distribution of citizen's charters by state and sector, design and content of the charters, access to and awareness about the charters, modalities of implementation, and impact on service delivery were analysed in terms of both strengths and weaknesses. Firstly, the study raised fundamental questions of the strategies adopted by the GoI to promote citizen's charters. There was clearly no momentum built within the government, initially to motivate and equip both government leaders and staff to design and deliver services effectively, while preparing the ground to introduce formal citizen's charters. Government adopted citizen's charters implementation, at one go, for all the departments instead they could have implemented in a phased manner. For example, some agencies may need more time to specify and agree upon realistic standards of service. In others, additional effort will be required to motivate and equip the staff to participate in this reform exercise. Such organisations may be given time and resources to experiment with standards, grievance redress mechanisms or training. They may also need more time for internal restructuring of the service delivery chain or introducing new systems.

The study also highlighted the fact that there was considerable scope for the creative use of e-governance methods to make government systems more efficient and transparent. In such cases, formal citizen's charters could have been adopted and publicised only after these prerequisites are fully in place. Training and build capacity internally to implement the programme has been another area where the government could not focus well. There was no adequate consultation with staff and citizen groups for internalising the process. The quality of citizen's charters developed by the departments was also questioned and the need for systematic monitoring and review of citizen's charters was emphasised. The need for making citizen's charter design and implementation a mandatory milestone reflecting the performance of officials in the government was recommended in the study as this would bring more seriousness in charter implementation.

In 2008, a review by the Second Administrative Reforms Commission was conducted on charter implementation and a number of challenges in the implementation of citizen's charters were highlighted.[1] It was found that almost 41 per cent of the Charters under consideration did not indicate any time frame for redressing of public grievances. Sixty-one per cent of them did not indicate any time frame for acknowledging the receipt of public grievances and nearly 43 per cent of them did not have the time frame for responding to the petitioners. None of the charters reviewed specified whether a petitioner would be conveyed the reasons for rejection of his grievance, nor did these charters mandate any penalties against the government or its officials if they were violated. This was a major indication of the problems in the implementation of citizen's charter programme in India.

In order to strengthen the citizen's charter implementation, to bridge the gaps left by the citizen's charters and to strengthen service delivery through a legislative process, the Right to Public Service Act was brought in by various state governments in India. The act provides for a legal mandate to the process of service delivery and ensures to all the citizens on timely service delivery while directing the provider to cover all services clearly stating the specific timelines for service delivery within a specific time frame. The act envisages penalties against the responsible officer if they do not complete the service within the time frame. The inspiration to fine the responsible officer for poor implementation has been derived from the provisions of the RTI Act 2005. In a nutshell, the Right to Public Service is a statutory law which guarantees time bound delivery of services for various public services rendered by the government to the citizens and provides mechanisms for punishing the errant public servants that are

---

1. 12th Report by Second Administrative Reforms Committee, *Report on Citizen Centric Administration*, New Delhi, 2009.

Table 3.1

Various States which have Implemented the Public Service Delivery Acts

S.No.	*Title of the Act*	*State*	*Date of Implementation*
1	The Madhya Pradesh Lok Sewaon Ke Pradan Ki Guarantee Adhiniyam	Madhya Pradesh	August 18, 2010
2	The Uttar Pradesh Janhit Guarantee Adhyadesh	Uttar Pradesh	January 13, 2011
3	The Delhi (Right of Citizen to Time Bound Delivery of Services) Act, 2011	Delhi	April 28, 2011
4	The Jammu and Kashmir Public Services Guarantee Act, 2011	Jammu and Kashmir	April 13, 2011
5	Bihar Right to Public Services Act, 2011	Bihar	August 15, 2011
6	The Rajasthan Guaranteed Delivery of Public Services Act, 2011	Rajasthan	September 21, 2011
7	The Uttarakhand Right to Service Act, 2011	Uttarakhand	October 04, 2011
8	Himachal Pradesh Public Services Guarantee Act, 2011	Himachal Pradesh	October 17, 2011
9	The Punjab Right to Service Act, 2011	Punjab	October 20, 2011
10	The Jharkhand Right to Service Act, 2011	Jharkhand	November 15, 2011
11	Kerala Government Service Assurance Bill	Kerala	2011
11	Karnataka Right of Citizens to Time Bound Delivery of Services Bill	Karnataka	2011
12	Chhattisgarh Lok Seva Guarantee Bill	Chhattisgarh	2011
13	Jammu and Kashmir Public Services Guarantee Act	Jammu and Kashmir	2011
14	Odisha Right to Public Services Act	Odisha	2012
15	Assam Right to Public Services Act	Assam	2012
17	Gujarat Right of Citizens to Public Services Bill	Gujarat	2013
18	West Bengal Right to Public Services Bill	West Bengal	2013

Source: Mathur, 2012.

deficient in providing the service stipulated under the statute. This act has a mandate to check corrupt practices among the government officials and to enhance transparency and public accountability.

In India, more than 15 states have enacted the Public Service Legislation. Madhya Pradesh (MP) is the first state in India to enact Right to Service Act in 2010 followed by Bihar which enacted this bill in July 2011. Table 3.1 indicates the states covered under the Public Service Delivery Act.

The scope of the Act varies from state to state while the overall aim has been to provide time-bound services to the citizens and provide for redressal of citizens' grievances through an institutional mechanism and in case of failure to provide services, clear penalties are imposed on the defaulting officer or for compensation due to the appellant in case of failure in service delivery. Table 3.2 highlights the implementation status in different states with regard to issues such as, the department responsible for implementing the act, number of services notified under the act, penalty provisions, monitoring mechanisms and use of technology, etc.

In the next section, we will discuss the implementation experiences of states like MP, Kerala, Bihar and Karnataka with their respective Public Service Delivery Acts. These states have clearly received support from top political leadership and also the bureaucratic support for implementation of the act.

Implementation Experiences of Few States

Experience of Madhya Pradesh

MP was the first state to pass its Public Service Guarantee Act in August 2010. Many of the states modelled their acts on the lines of MP. The act covers 52 services of the government provided by various departments. The act mandates the designated official of the department to provide the service to the citizen on request or deny the service through a written explanation. The allotted time in the act within which action has to be taken on request ranges somewhere between 3 and 60 days depending on the type of service requested. If the designated official fails to provide the required response to the citizen, there is a provision in the act where the applicant can appeal to a designated officer. In MP, the District Collector at the district level and a sub-divisional officer at the sub-district level are the responsible appellate authorities. These officials decide the appeal within a stipulated period of time and can order the appropriate public official to provide the service. The decision of the appeal officer can be further appealed to a second appellate officer usually a higher level official than the first appellate officer. The second appellate officer may fine the designated public official between ₹500 and ₹5000, if they feel that the officer has failed to comply with the provision of the act without any reasonable cause. The first appeal officer could also face a penalty/fine if it is observed that he/she has failed to decide on the case within the stipulated time period without a reasonable cause.

The Department of Public Service Management is the nodal agency which monitors the implementation of the act in MP. Each district is manned by a manager and a computer assistant both of whom are jointly responsible to support the implementation. The team ensures that the act is implemented by departments as per the stipulations. They ensure the proper upkeep of records and ensure that services are offered in the stipulated time period. A study taken up by the Centre for Policy Research, New Delhi, has reported that in order to ensure effective implementation of the act, the state government has undertaken process simplification including simplifying the application forms/formats/procedures (Robinson, 2013).

Experience of Bihar

The Government of Bihar implemented the Right to Public Service Act in the year 2011. The Act covers 50 public services provided by various departments. The General Administration department is the nodal agency in Bihar which is implementing the Act. The state government received funding assistance from the UK-based funding agency Department for International Development (DFID) for the implementation of the act.

In order to effectively implement the act, various centres have been created in each block, and similar to MP, a dedicated team supports the implementation of the act at the district level. Front

Table 3.2

Variations in Provisions of the Act in Different State Governments

State Responsible	*Authority*	*Services Notified*	*Penalty Provisions*	*Monitoring Mechanism*	*Use of ICT Tools*
Madhya Pradesh	Department of Public Service Management	52 services from 16 departments	₹250 per day up to a maximum of INR 5000	Chief Minister's Office and online tracking System	Online application and tracking system through MIS
Bihar	Implemented under the Bihar Prashasanik Sudhar Mission	50 services from 10 departments	₹250 per day up to a maximum of INR 5000	Extensive ICT-based system Adhikaar Samadhan and Jigyasa for monitoring at the state, district and block levels	Computerized application and monitoring system
Jammu and Kashmir	Designated Officers (DOs), First Appellate Officers (FAOs) in respective departments	45 services from 6 departments	₹250 per day up to a maximum of INR 5000	Monitoring by the implementing officials	Applications being developed
Delhi	Department of Information and Technology	52 services from 18 departments	₹10 per day up to a maximum of INR 200	e-Service Level Agreement Software Monitoring System in place	Complete ICT-based system for filing application and tracking status.
Jharkhand	DOs, FAOs and Second Appellate Officers (SAOs) in respective departments	54 services from 20 departments	₹250 per day up to a maximum of INR 5000	Development under process	Development under Process

contd...

...contd...

Haryana	DOs, FAOs and SAOs in respective departments	36 services from 8 Departments	At the moment no provisions to penalise, any feedback to be included in annual performance reports	Frequent visits of deputy commissioners to public dealing offices, DOs also responsible for monitoring	Software for application and tracking developed by an external agency, full roll out in the pipeline
Karnataka	Department of General Administration/Mission Director Sakala	265 services covering 19 departments	Any delayed disposal entitles the citizen to receive Compensatory Cost (@ ₹20 per day, ₹500 max)	District Magistrate is the Chief Nodal officer at the district level who oversees the implementation of the act	Complete ICT-based system for filing application and tracking status.
Kerala	Personnel and Administrative Reforms	A total of 151 services in 11 major government departments	Ranging from ₹500 to 5000 or may recommend disciplinary proceedings	The first appeal officer, second appellate authority, and above them the government appointed officers.	-

Source: One World Foundation (2011).

desks/information desks have been set up where people are available to provide information and accept the applications from citizens under the Right to Public Service Act. They also provide the citizen's with a computer generated receipt as an acknowledgement. The receipt details out the number of days in which the service will be delivered to the citizen. Government of Bihar provides for a single window counter, wherein the applications are submitted in the morning and by the end of the day they are handed over after processing. Officials in the district headquarters monitor the progress and status of applications which are accepted and the disposal of applications on a daily basis. A study done by the Centre for Policy Research observed that in the past few years of implementation of the Right to Public Service Act, in Bihar, though there are some appeals received from citizens, the cases of penalisation have been rare (Robinson, 2013). The act being very new, many of the state governments are still in the process of getting their systems stabilised both in terms of supply side and demand side of the service delivery. The provider side issues being that the staff and employees responsible for accepting the applications are still not abiding by the timelines and there are very few instances wherein penalties and compensations are being paid by them for non-delivery of services.

It was found in the study that in 2011 (about a year after it was enacted) less than 2 per cent of the applicants covered under various services had awareness about the act and its provisions. There was also lack of knowledge on the process to be adopted in case services were not provided by the agency. In fact, people did not know about the appeal mechanism in place and the appellate authorities that had to be contacted for registering their grievances. As it had happened with the implementation of RTI Act 2005, wherein information sought from various offices included only those applicants who were employees and wanted to get details on the seniority list and transfer guidelines etc from the departments. In the implementation of the Right to Public Service Act also it appears as if the service provider is getting acclimatised to various service provisions and timelines for service delivery within the system, but is not getting down to the citizens at large and their awareness levels still remains very poor on the provisions of the act.

A survey done by the Bihar government reported that the menace of middlemen has reduced with the implementation of the act (Mathur, 2012). The study shows that in Bihar and MP, there have been marked changes observed in service delivery processes and computerisation has brought about a major shift, making processes more transparent and enhancing accountability of officials has improved tremendously. But at the same time, the study also highlights another problem, which has come up due to fixing timelines for service delivery, officials are waiting to deliver a particular listed service delivery till the final stipulated timeline is completed and they are not trying to complete the work as and when they get the application. This has become a major drawback in the implementation of the act. The study also reveals that officials responsible for implementation of the act felt that processing applications under this act is consuming a lot of time of the officials and they are not able to complete their other regular jobs on time. Therefore, what we may infer from the above is that, with the implementation of the act at least the system has been put on an alert and slowly and steadily things will start to fall in line.

Experience of Kerala

Government of Kerala has been pro-active on a number of fronts to make governance pro-citizens. Government of Kerala was the first government to give a statutory status to citizen's charter implementation in the country. The Kerala Municipality Act of 1994 made it mandatory for all the municipalities to formulate and design citizen's charters giving details of services along with specified procedures. It is a known fact that citizens of Kerala get several services from various Government offices, but as any other state, they have their set of problems of meeting scheduled timelines and providing efficient service delivery. As a step to solve the problems faced by citizens to access government services and to put in place an effective law to guarantee such services in a time-bound manner on lines of the RTI Act, the Kerala Right to Service Act was enacted by the state government in 2011.

The act makes it mandatory for the government officials to provide particular services to citizens within a stipulated period of time. Services which are included in the act are distribution of birth, death and income certificates, electricity connection, social security pensions, assistance for victims of natural disasters and a few other services that have been made a part of the legislation.

The key points of the Kerala Government Service Assurance Act, 2011, include:

- Provides right to citizens to get service within stipulated time limit from a designated public officer in the department.
- Any person whose application is rejected or who is not provided with service within a stipulated time limit can file an appeal within 30 days.
- If the appellate officer finds that the public officer has failed in his duties to provide service without sufficient and reasonable cause to the appellant, he may impose a lump sum penalty not be less than ₹250 and not more than ₹25,000. This penalty amount is deducted from the salary of the designated officer responsible for service delivery.

Experience of Karnataka

The Government of Karnataka has successfully implemented the Karnataka Sakala Services Act in the year 2011 in order to make the service delivery more accessible to its citizens. The act mandates government departments to deliver services within a stipulated period of time. Under this act around 419 services have been identified under 42 different departments. Karnataka has become the first state to offer the maximum variety of services under this scheme. In an effort to further enrich the process, the government has brought in the computerised service delivery model and is offering around 69 services online to the citizens. The act also makes it mandatory for the departments to deliver the notified services within a stipulated time. In case of non-compliance like the RTI Act, this act also evokes a penal provision and the applicant shall be paid compensation and the money will be recovered from the officials responsible. In case the application is rejected or if the service is not provided within the stipulated time, citizens can file an appeal before the CO (competent officer) to redress their grievance. The competent officer will hear the appeal and redress the grievance within the specified time. Citizens can claim in cash the compensatory cost of ₹20 per day for the delayed period subject to a maximum of ₹500 from the CO, upfront. The same shall be deducted from the salary of the designated officer or his subordinate responsible for delay or default, within 30 days (Rajneesh, 2012).

In order to effectively implement the act, a mission has been constituted by the Government to assist the Department of Administrative Reforms. This mission is led by a Senior IAS (Indian Administrative Service) officer as ex-officio Mission Director with a support team. Funds have been allocated for the pilot projects being taken up which takes care of the infrastructure development for implementation of the project like hardware, software, capacity building, etc. Around 36,000 designated officials have been trained regarding the provisions of the act and the training is a continuous process. Training was especially imparted on soft skills for bringing about attitudinal changes. Sarvottam Seva Cash awards have been instituted to recognise and encourage those employees who have been able to deliver services on time and have brought in innovations in their operations.

Use of IT (information technology) is being done in a big way for implementation of the project. A comprehensive portal *www.sakala.nic.in* has been developed which provides all the required information to citizens on this project. Through this website, citizens can send in their applications to the concerned officials for selected services. There are pre-designed formats which are made available on the website to the citizen for accessing services, details of services along with timelines, contact details of persons responsible for service delivery, appeal process, and FAQs, etc., are made available on the website. The portal also assists the service provider to monitor the process online including tracking of applications and ensuring that timelines for service delivery are met. This process provides a lot of transparency and accountability to the functioning of government. There is a 15 digit GSC (Guarantee of Services to Citizens) number, through which the citizen can monitor the status of his application through SMS (short message service) or on the website. The system provides for the monitoring officers to get daily reports on delays/rejections/pendency, so that they can take necessary action. Help desks at every district/*taluka* level have been established to ensure that citizens are facilitated through the government processes. A continuous monitoring is being done to ensure reengineering of redundant processes and bringing in smarter ways of working. Reputed organisations such as IIM Bangalore, The Karnataka Evaluation Authority (KEA), The University of Chicago, and 'Indian Market Research Bureau' (IMRB) have taken up the task of evaluating Sakala in a 360 degree evaluation methodology.

Proposed Legislation by Government of India

The citizen's charters have been recognised as a robust governance tool in the hands of citizens which has the capacity to induce greater accountability, transparency and responsiveness into the system and improve service delivery. The Union Cabinet in response to the demands from civil society groups and people of India, approved a bill on The Right of Citizen's for Time Bound Delivery of Goods and Services and Redressal of their Grievances Bill, 2011, in the year 2013 which has yet to receive the consent of President of India after which it becomes enforceable.

Key Highlights

The bill makes it obligatory for every public authority to publish citizen's charter, clearly stating the timelines within which specified goods shall be supplied and services be rendered and provide for a grievance redressal mechanism for non-compliance of the citizen's charter. The bill provides the right to every individual citizen of India to have the right to time bound delivery of goods and provision for services and redressal of grievances (Section 3).

Role of Public Authorities

Every public authority has to undertake certain mandatory activities:

- Every public authority is mandated to publish, within six months of the commencement of this Act, a citizen's charter specifying therein the category of goods supplied and services rendered by it, the time within which such goods shall be supplied or services be rendered, Section 4(1).

- The citizen's charters to consist of the following details, Section 4(2):
  - (i) Details of goods supplied and services rendered by the public authority and the name of person or agency through which such goods are supplied or services rendered and timings during which such services are supplied or services rendered.
  - (ii) Conditions under which a person becomes entitled for goods or services, and the class of persons who are entitled to receive such goods and avail services.
  - (iii) Quantitative and tangible parameters (including weight, size, frequency) of the goods and services available to the public.
  - (iv) Complaint redressal mechanism including the time within which the complaint be disposed of and the officer of the public authority to whom such complaint may be made.
  - (v) Name and addresses of individuals responsible for the delivery of goods or rendering of services mentioned in the charter.

If implemented in letter and spirit, these provisions will bring in greater transparency and accountability in the working of every public authority and empower the people of this country by sharing government-related information. These provisions also work complimentary to the provisions under the RTI Act 2005. With the public authorities providing information on their basic service delivery aspects, citizens will be better equipped to ask information on areas which make a difference in their day to day life.

Suggested Formats for Public Authorities

Format 1

S.No.	*Details of Goods and Services Rendered*	*Name of the Person/Agency Supplying Goods/Services*	*Timing for Service Delivery*

Format 2

Details of Goods and Services	*Persons Entitled to Avail the Service*	*Timings for Availing Service*	*Person Responsible to Deliver the Service in the Department*
Service 1			
Service 2			

Format 3

Details of Goods and Services	*Number of Times the Goods/Services are Made Available*	*How much Service will be Made Available*	*Person Responsible to Deliver the Service in the Department*
Service 1			
Service 2			

Format 4

S.No.	*Nature of Grievance/ Complaint*	*Timelines for Disposal of Complaint*	*Authority Responsible for Disposing off the Complaint*

Format 5

S.No.	*Responsibility of Public Authority*

Obligation of Head of Department(s) (Section 5)

The heads of the departments are mandated to do the following:

- Updating and verifying the accuracy of the contents of citizen's charter every year.
- Ensure that the citizen's charter is widely disseminated to the public.
- Take appropriate steps in accordance with section 4 of the RTI Act 2005 for providing relevant information to the public enabling them to exercise their rights.
- Ensure that all material is disseminated in the local language free of cost.

There is clarity in the bill regarding the expression 'disseminated' as making known and communicating the information to the public through notice boards, newspapers, public announcements, media broadcasts, the Internet or any other means, including inspection of offices of any public authority by any citizen.

- Ensure that the citizen's charter is made available at the website and in other electronic forms and shall be available free of cost.
- Ensure that a copy of the citizen's charter duly certified is submitted/made available to the Central and State Public Grievance Redress Commission.

Suggested Checklist of Activities

Action Points	*Done*	*To be Done*	*When Will it be Done?*
Displaying the charter in a prominent place in your office.			
Does every member of your office have a copy of the charter?			
Does your department have a website?			
Are copies of the charter freely available?			
Have you established call centres?			
Do you have an email response system?			

Establishment of Information and Facilitation Centres (IFCs) (Section 6)

The act directs the public authorities:

- To establish IFC for efficient and effective delivery of services and redressal of grievances, which may include establishment of customer care centre, call centre, help desk, peoples support centre.
- Take responsibility for the development, improvement, modernisation and reform in service delivery and redressal of grievance system, including adoption of electronic modes, Internet, etc.

How to Go About?

The biggest problem that people usually face with government offices is the number of people they need to meet to get a simple job done. Even something as common as obtaining approval for a building plan requires the document to pass through the hands of more than 50 government officials. Most people feel lost in a government office and often, several days go by before they are directed to the right person. In such a context, what is needed is an IFC. The essentials of an IFC are:

- The centre should be as near the entrance as possible and prominently sign-boarded.
- To provide information on services, schemes and procedures concerning the department.
- To provide all required forms used for various procedures.
- Contain brochures, booklets and reports that will give more information.
- Manned by competent employees who will personally or over the phone direct users to the correct officers or guide them on procedures and documentation required.
- IFC to receive complaints and also issue acknowledgement slips indicating the section dealing with the subject.

- IFC to provide all forms and materials required by subscribers and act as a single window help desk.

Grievance Redress Officers (including Municipalities and *Panchayat*) (Section 7)

The act envisions placing a grievance redress officer(s) in all the administrative units of the public authority at central, state, district and sub-district levels, municipalities, *panchayats* within six months from the date of the coming into force of this act:

- Wide publicity to be given to this matter wherein, the name of the Grievance Redress Officer, his address and telephone number, e-mail address, facsimile number and other means of contacting him to be widely published through public notice-newspapers in local language. Any change in name, address or any other details regular updation to be carried out by the public authority from time to time.
- Name of the Grievance Redress Officer with address and telephone numbers, e-mail addresses, facsimile numbers and other contact details to be made available at IFCs, call centre, customer care centre, help desk, and at the sales outlets, and websites.
- The Grievance Redress Officer is mandated to provide all necessary assistance to citizens in filing complaints. Where a complainant is unable to make a complaint in writing, the Grievance Redress Officer to render all reasonable assistance to the person making the request orally to reduce the same in writing.

Some Useful Tips!

- Select an officer on the basis of a careful assessment of his/her attitude and suitability for the job, because grievance redressal process needs the right attitude for the person involved in the function.
- Train and sensitise the officer adequately to undertake the job.

- Sensitise the other employees to cooperate with him in undertaking his duties and responsibilities.
- Involve the officer actively in the process of formulation and implementation of citizen's charter at each and every stage.
- Prepare a detailed job chart for the officer for greater clarity of his role.

Acknowledgement (Section 8)

The act provides for all complaints to be acknowledged within two days of the making of the complaint, by a receipt, issued in writing or through electronic means or through text message or through telephone or through any other means as may be prescribed, specifying the date, time, place, unique complaint number and particulars of receiver of complaint along with the stipulated time-frame in accordance with its citizen's charter within which the complaint will be redressed.

Note: Looking at the timelines given for acknowledgement, it is advised that the departments are ready with a format for acknowledging various types of complaints.

Acknowledgement to Complaint/Grievance

S. No. of the Complaint:
Date of Receiving the Complaint:
Name of the Complainant:
Registered Number:

Name & Designation of the Complaint Officer

Signature

Note: Grievance Redress Officers must maintain registers for complaints and parallel also update the information on computer so that there are better chances for simultaneous monitoring at various levels.

Report Requirements (Section 10)

The Grievance Redressal Officer is to prepare a fortnightly report with nature of complaints received, complaints redressed, reasons for complaints not being redressed to the Head of the Department of the Public Authority.

Suggested Format

For Internal Use
Date of Receiving the Complaint:
Name of the Complainant:
Registered Number:
Forwarded to:
Action Taken:
Further Action Required:
Name & Designation of the Officer
Signature

The act provides for an establishment of institutional machinery at the Central and state Levels. A Central Public Grievance Redressal Commission and a State Public Grievance Redressal Commission has been provided by the act consisting of a Chief Public Grievance Redress Commissioner (S31)/State Public Grievance Redress Commissioner (S29), and other Commissioners, not exceeding 10/5 out of which at least one each shall be from amongst scheduled castes (SCs), scheduled tribes (STs) and women.

Penalties and Compensation (Section 45)

The act provides for a penalty to be imposed by the State Public Grievance Redressal Commission or Central Public Grievance Redressal Commission, of a lump-sum amount against designated officials responsible for delivery of goods and service or Grievance Redress Officers for failure to deliver goods or render services to which the applicant is entitled, up to ₹50,000 which shall be recovered from the salary of the official against whom penalty has been imposed. A disciplinary action has also been proposed against the public servant if he is found guilty of a *mala fide* action in respect of any provision of this act.

Conclusion

Public service delivery acts have come into existence after almost a decade of experience in implementation of citizen's charters in the country. All the gaps that were seen in the charter implementation were designed to be plugged in these acts. With many states almost with more than 3-4 years of implementation experiences with the public service delivery act; what we can see is that there is a mixed reaction emerging from various studies that have been done so far. Although the initial gaps from the citizen's charter stage have been more or less taken care of in the act, there seems to be still a long way to go in terms of monitoring and strengthening implementation.

References

Parigi, V.K. and P. Geeta (2002). *A Guide to Developing and Implementing Citizen's Charter*. Centre for Good Governance, Government of Andhra Pradesh.

Public Affairs Centre (2007). *India's Citizen's Charter: A Decade of Experience*. Bangalore.

Robinson, Nick (2013). *Right to Public Services Act in India: The Experience of Bihar and Madhya Pradesh*. New Delhi: Centre for Policy Research.

Mathur, Tina (2012). *A Comparative Study on the Implementation of Public Service Delivery Acts in Select States in India*. A Project Report, Centre for Organisation Development.

One World Foundation (2011). *Strengthening Delivery and Accountability Frameworks for Public Services*. Project Report, Funded by UNDP.

Rajneesh, Shalini (2012). *A Presentation on Sakala- Public Service Delivery Act in Karnataka*. Secretary, Department of Public Administrative Reforms, Government of Karnataka.

4

Grievance Redressal Management System

Most dissatisfied citizens/clients do not complain because they think it's not worth the time and effort; they don't know how or where to complain!!!

The GRMS (Grievance Redressal Management System) has, very much, been a part of the Indian governance system for time immemorial. The GRMS that has existed in the districts and local governments in India for the last two decades is the normal traditional system based on the procedures laid down in the District Office Manual (DOM) which details out the procedure for dealing with any letters, weather petitions or other letters as fresh currents to be registered in the personal registers or filled in the existing files on the subject. It has been observed that all the procedures that have been laid down in the DOM were slowly discarded and were not being followed. This gave rise to a strange situation wherein *Pairavi* and *Pairavikars* system emerged which had middlemen who manage the problems of people in a community. Small time community leaders organise petitions on some common subjects to go and present collectively. Sometimes local or even sometime state level leaders intervene in the resolution of the petitions. In this scenario, the well-established system of grievance redressal and officials interface with the citizens in the districts and villages was practically absent, and there was no substitute to the old system. The authority of the district collector also came under a major threat with the *panchayati raj* system taking strong roots in India. But unfortunately the devolution of powers to *panchayats* also did not materialise in most of the states and there was no alternative available at the grass-roots level. This made the citizen run from pillar to post from office to office to get his/her grievances resolved.

The timelines for delivering public services has been a major issue of contention in public and has generated the maximum number of grievances. Generally, in government, when grievances emerge with regard to a specific department, it has to invariably be referred to the lowest levels of administration and then it moves through the proper channel to the district level administration and if required to the state level for resolution. The petitioner also has to make a number of visits to the offices at all these levels to push his case forward towards resolution. This system provides an opportunity for corruption and nepotism and also leads to great amount of public dissatisfaction. The other major reason for grievances is that the norms set by government departments for providing services are usually not adhered to by the service provider in many cases and their rules and regulations are archaic in nature. Slackness in administration, low morale of the services, inherent inertia, absence of incentives, lack of proper accountability and delay in decision making are other major factors which generate grievances in citizens. These factors need to be tackled properly through systematic changes. The grievances could also be related to a behavioural aspect of a person working in the office which has to be taken into cognisance.

Another set of factors responsible for generating grievances in the public/citizens needs to also be discussed at this juncture. It is a known fact that the general public many a times does not have the information and knowledge of the services being delivered by various government departments. This is the primary cause of generating grievances. There are many reasons for this including illiteracy, apathy, poverty and other causes.

Initiatives by Government

In recent years, a pattern has emerged in most of the governments departments, that one day of the week is exclusively earmarked to be spent by responsible officials in an organisation, to meet the public/citizen and listen to their grievances. In fact, the chief minister(s) or minister(s) in many state governments also organise special tour programmes to meet the people and listen from them on what programmes have not worked and which of the programmes have worked well (Griglani, 2006). It is a routine in government offices for every day officers to listen to different types of grievances from the public/citizens on issues that affect their well being.

One of the key ingredients of the citizen's charter programme is to establish a culture of accountability, transparency, responsiveness and participation. Citizen's charter as we have seen in the earlier chapters is a written declaration by the government department, which highlights the standards of service delivery and inculcates a culture of accountability in the working of the organisation and makes the functioning of the organisation more transparent to the general public. As per the guidelines provided by the Performance Management division for developing citizen's charter for a ministry/ department, setting up a grievance redressal mechanism is one of the nine key elements to be present in the charter.[1]

Grievance redressal mechanism is an integral component of the charter programme. The Government of India (GoI) guidelines on citizen's charter define grievances as expressions of resentment against specific acts of omission or commission that are wrong or perceived as wrong, and requiring corrective action to be taken. In case the citizens who don't get the services from a particular organisation as assured by them within the stipulated period of time, there has to be a mechanism where he/she can register the grievances. Therefore, a grievance redressal mechanism needs to be established by organisations so that people have access to some point where they can register their grievances that will ultimately be redressed. The citizen's charter also creates an avenue for establishing a mechanism of grievance redressal. The process or mechanisms set up by organisations to receive records, investigate, redress, analyse, prevent or take any other appropriate action in respect of grievances lodged against them is called GRMs (Grievance Redress Mechanisms).[2]

Traditionally, the grievance redressal mechanisms in departments/ ministries have been handled through manual mechanisms through registers. These registers are used for recording the written complaints received and later forwarded to the respective units for

1. Guidelines on Citizens' Charters released by the Performance Management Division, Cabinet Secretariat.

2. Ibid.

action. Currently, with the availability of computerised systems, it has become possible to maintain such systems centrally so that grievances can be managed with some uniformity even across large, decentralised organisations. More importantly, it has become possible for the citizens/clients to lodge grievances from the comfort of their homes or offices without having to visit any office specially for lodging a grievance. One such system extensively being used in the Central government ministries/departments is the CPGRAMS (Centralised Public Grievance Redress and Monitoring System).[3] The citizens can also lodge their grievances from any internet facility on *www.pgportal.nic.in*.

The Department of Administrative Reforms and Public Grievances (DARPG) is the nodal agency for policy formulation on grievance handling. Establishing a grievance redressal system can set in the culture of accountability, transparency and responsiveness in the working of government agencies and goes a long way in establishing good governance.

Essentials of a Grievance Redressal System

For a grievance redressal system to be efficient, it must be a simple system, easily accessible and well publicised. The department must be open to receive complainants and provide information about how to make a complaint and who to approach; the department must make this common knowledge. The complaint processes must be user-friendly and easy to use. Complaints must be dealt with quickly with reasonable time limits set for each stage of the process. Complainants must be kept informed about progress. Ideally, the front-line staff must have the authority to deal with complaints at first contact instead of passing it on to a series of people. Published standards: speedy, with established time limits for action and keeping people informed of progress. Without a good complaint redressal system/grievance redressal system, citizen's charters have no effect. Departments should establish highly credible and responsive complaints procedures and redressal systems.

3. Ibid.

Steps for Grievance Redress

In this section, the various steps to be followed for designing a grievance redressal mechanism in an organisation have been discussed.[4]

Step 1: Identifying the Need for a Grievance Redressal System

In order to resolve a grievance, the very first step is to identify the real issue, in the context of the rules and regulatory framework of the department. It is important to address some of the questions such as: did the organisation violate any of its mandated provisions, a rule or regulation, a policy or procedure, or any practice? Did the organisation give an unfair treatment to any individual? Did the organisation create situations where the citizen felt discriminated or harassed? Did the organisation take any disciplinary action against an employee or group of employees for not having solving the grievance of the citizens? If the answer to any of these questions is 'yes,' there is a good chance that grounds for a grievance may exist.

There is a need to develop robust systems and procedures for handling grievances within the departments. Each department should have procedures on dealing with grievances which are clearly understood and followed by the staff. The procedures should be simple and enable speedy solutions to the complaint received.

Step 2: Receive and Acknowledge Citizen Grievances

Every department is responsible for being concerned about the citizens and must receive their grievances personally by the complainant or received by post. There should be a designated place, person and time to receive these complaints. Persons specifically assigned for this work must be a part of the Information and Facilitation Counters at the reception. The person should be responsible for receiving the grievances, issuing the acknowledgement receipt simultaneously and maintain the record in the format given below. To ensure that all relevant particulars of the individual

4. *Formulating a Grievance Redressal Mechanism for Local Self Government Institutions in Kerala*, A Report Submitted by Centre for Good Governance, Hyderabad to Government of Kerala under the modernising governance programme, 2007.

A Sample Format

#	Date of Receipt	*Particulars of Citizen/Client*				*Particulars of the Grievance*			
		Name	*Address*	*Landline/ Mobile/ Email*	*Whether Acknowledgement Given at the Time of Receipt*	*Subject of the Grievance*	*Office*	*Brief Description*	*Date of Acknowledgement Date of Redress*
1	2	3	4	5	6 (Yes / No)	7	8	9	10

registering the complaint are available for further actions to be taken, full details must be recorded at the time of receiving a grievance or complaint.

At the time of acknowledgement, the complainant should be provided with the following information:

- Grievance number to facilitate monitoring and reminders by complainants.
- Expected time of redress (prescribed maximum time limit for completion of redress is three months).
- If not addressed within expected time, action to be taken by complainant.

If the grievance is not redressed within the expected time, the complainant should be provided with the following information by the person responsible for receiving the manual/postal grievances:

- Information on reasons for delay.
- Updated expected time of redress.
- If not addressed within expected time, action to be taken by complainant.

At the time of final redress, the complainant should be provided with the following information by the office responsible for redress of the grievances:

- Action taken for redress.
- If not satisfied with the redress action, avenues for pursuing the matter further.

The information should be given in the same letter/order through which the final decision on redress is conveyed to the complainant.

Step 3: Setting up Information and Facilitation Centres (IFC)

An integral aspect of administrative reforms both in the short term and in the longer perspective is related to the speedy and easy access of information to the public on the services and activities of government. There are considerable delays in redressal of grievances and securing access to information, since government departments with a public service interface do not have a mechanism to provide information to the citizens across the counter or to deal with their queries and complaints at a single point. The guidelines on citizen's charter released by GoI, directs all government departments and agencies to set up IFCs. All guidelines on citizen's/client's charter including duties of Nodal Officer for citizen's/client's charter are available on DARPG website *www.darpg.nic.in*, in the "Compilation of Guidelines for Redress of Public Grievances 2010".

The compilation of Guidelines for Redress of Public Grievances 2010 contains all the major guidelines issued since 1985 for the creation of grievance redress mechanism in all ministries/departments/organisations of GoI. The compilation also includes separate sections containing all the original orders issued since 1997 on citizen's/client charter and Information Facilitation counters in GoI as well as state governments/union territories (UTs) administrations. So far 105 ministries/departments/organisations have set up IFCs/'May I Help You'/'Enquiry Counters.' These ministries/departments/organisations have designated a senior officer as contact officer who is overall incharge of the IFC and can be contacted in case of any difficulty or feedback.

Salient Features

The IFCs provide information regarding services, schemes and procedure through brochures, booklets, reports, etc. Provide information regarding position of waiting lists and applications through computer screens updated every day and through computerised query to departmental data base.

- Provide information regarding matters such as bill payments, registrations, land/house allotment, etc., over the phone or personally to the public.
- Forms which are to be utilised for various procedures should be available at the facilitation centre, even if the processing is to be done elsewhere.
- Receive complaints, issue acknowledgement slips indicating the section dealing with the complaints.
- A sufficiently senior officer is to man the facilitation centres with appropriate orientation, capable of speaking English

and local language for handling customers and knowledge of use of computers. Time limits and other details should be notified through display boards at the facilitation centres for completion of various procedures and for disposal of cases.

- Ensure easy accessibility to facilitation centres for the customer and average citizen and publicity regarding the location and hours of access.
- Utilising Interactive Voice System where feasible for enquiry response.

Duties and Responsibilities of the Contact Officers of IFCs

The contact officer of the information and facilitation counter is the overall in charge of the unit and is the link between the IFC and the mother organisation. He/she has to assess the information needs of the clients, create the corresponding supporting system at IFC, arrange the posting of suitable personnel and also to motivate them for the assigned job. Therefore, it is imperative that a senior level officer not below the rank of deputy secretary, director should be nominated as the contact officer and he/she should be reporting to the head of the department directly. The duties and responsibilities of the contact officers would be as under, in addition to the duties and responsibilities of the post that he/she is holding.

Planning

- The contact officer acts as a link between the IFC and the mother organisation and project the role of IFC before the senior management.
- He/she identifies the clients and assesses their information needs/possible queries, initially on the basis of substantive functions of the organisation and subsequently on the basis of analysis of the visitors' queries.
- He/she plans the infrastructure requirements at the counter, visualises the scope of work and facilitates flow of information to and from the IFC.

- He/she takes steps to create public awareness about existence of IFC through adequate publicity.

Organising

As an organiser, the role of the contact officer will be:

- To assess the manpower requirement with job profiles, to identify suitable personnel, preferably the willing ones, for IFC and to arrange their posting.
- To provide proper orientation and motivation to the personnel by clarifying the importance of their work at IFC and its contribution in building the image of the organisation.
- To identify the training needs of the functionaries at IFC and arrange suitable training programmes in behavioural skills, computer operation and other areas of operation.
- To ensure availability of necessary tools like computer, telephone, basic amenities like drinking water/toilet facilities, proper sitting space for visitors, etc.
- To install proper feedback mechanism through visitors' register/suggestion box and inviting suggestions from NGOs etc.
- To ensure proper signage indications for easy access to the IFC.

Controlling

The Contact Officer will be controller of the IFC mechanism and his role in the capacity would be as under:

- To ensure upkeep and tidiness at the counter.
- To ensure punctuality and discipline among the personnel.
- To ensure availability of relevant information material like annual report, brochures of schemes, projects of the organisation, periodicals, booklets, citizen's charter, Departmental Telephone Directory, list of officers dealing with substantive functions along with their telephone numbers, copies of departmental instructions, list of priced publications along with the details of outlets, applications forms of public usage, etc.

- To ensure that IFC is included in the organisation's mailing lists and all the circulars, etc., on policy changes of general interests are sent to the recipients of the mailing list.
- To attend to the day-to-day problems/personal needs of the staff.
- To ensure timely submission of periodical reports/returns by IFC.

Supervising

The contact officer will perform the following functions in the capacity of the supervising officer:

- Keeping track of complaints/grievances.
- To scrutinise the visitor register every week.
- To analyse the suggestions/feedback received through the suggestion box or visitors register, and initiate corrective action.
- To conduct surprise/periodical visits at the counter to see the mannerism and behaviour of the personnel manning IFC.
- To ensure that the telephone queries are being attended to with courtesy and their record is being maintained.
- To see that the names and telephone numbers of director of grievances and the contact officer are displayed prominently.
- To arrange visits of the senior officers to the counter.
- To arrange annual O&M inspection of the IFC.
- To arrange for wide and regular publicity of the IFC in media.

Grievances are an indicator of the agency's health and the departments are required to regularly keep analysing the complaints that emerge on a regular basis. For this purpose, a monitoring mechanism is suggested to be put in place, which will lead to understanding the problems and providing solutions for any systemic changes necessary for the department based on the analysis and lead to simplification or improvement of procedures.

Documentation

It is a well-known fact that government agencies do not focus on documenting complaints that were received by public. Documentation of complaints must be done so that it can be analysed to find the right solutions. It will also help the agency to narrow down on persons who don't perform, or identify bottlenecks in service delivery and rectify recurring or systemic problems. Prompt grievance redressal goes a long way in building credibility among your customers. A recommended menu of redress options could be:

- An apology.
- An explanation.
- Assurance that the same thing will not happen again, backed up by action and monitoring.
- Action taken to put things right.
- Financial compensation.

There are many ways an agency may handle complaints. But it is a fact that no organisation would like to receive a complaint. After putting in great efforts to provide good service, it leaves a bad feeling to know that there is someone out there who is registering their displeasure. Most people react emotionally to complaints because they feel they are being blamed. However, the truth is that not everyone complains. Most people, when they find something wanting in the service, shrug and leave the matter there. Only a few take the trouble to pick up the phone or pen to inform or raise their voice for the agency to know the issue. Agencies must look at as an opportunity to fix the issue or the problem. So whenever an agency receives complaints, it is advisable that they listen to the message, not the tone.

Criteria for Classification: GoI has issued guidelines on classification of complaints. Different types of grievances or complaints need different responses or ways to respond to them. Therefore, the grievance must be categorised to facilitate action appropriate to the type of grievance. The DARPG has provided five broad suggestive criteria under which the ministry/department can categorise their grievances. These five criteria can be listed in the following format:

S.No.	Criteria	Grievance Category
1.	Charter related	
2.	Policy related	
3.	Personnel related	
4.	Pensioners' related	
5.	Vigilance related	

Time Norms for Redress: Based on the criteria listed as above time norms for redress must be laid down as shown below:

S.No.	Grievance Category	Time Norm for Redress

Level of Responsibility for Redress: In order to ensure that grievances are addressed within the prescribed time norms, the GRM should define the levels of responsibility for redress of each category of grievances and their time norms. In case the grievance is not redressed at a particular defined level, then an avenue should be available to the complainant to approach the next higher authority. The responsible officials at each level should alert their next superior official well in time if a grievance is likely to exceed the prescribed time norm. The next higher authority should call for a report to redress escalated grievances.

They can then take appropriate action without the complainant having to repeatedly remind or pursue the issue. The table for level of responsibility for redress must contain the following information as applicable:

S.No.	Type of Grievance	Time Line for Redress at Level 1	Time Line for Level 2	Time Line for Level 3	Time Line for Level 4

Analysis and Prevention: Grievances can be viewed as free inputs to the organisations, to understand the expectations of service recipients better and initiate systemic reforms to meet those expectations. Ministries/departments must analyse why they are receiving particular types of grievances more frequently than others. Such grievance-prone areas need to be identified and analysed for bringing about necessary changes proactively.

A format for root cause analysis of grievance prone areas is as follows:

S.No.	*Date and description of Grievance*	*Grievance-Prone Areas Identified*	*Root Cause Identified*	*Action Required to Improve System*	*Planned Date and Authority Responsible for Taking Action*	*Action Taken Date*

Review and Monitoring of Grievance Redress Mechanism

GoI has issued guidelines for review. The ministry/department should have a system in place to call for monthly reports on grievance redress from responsibility centres. The report should also contain information regarding the status of unaddressed/unresolved grievances. In case of an automated system, the monthly report should be able to automatically generate this information. All ministries/departments should also consolidate the grievances redressed and pending at their own level on a monthly basis. The Director of Public Grievances of the ministry/department should review the grievances pending at their own level and with the responsibility centres periodically.

Feedback from Citizens

Another important prerequisite is getting feedback from citizens on various aspects of service delivery as well as aspects of the redressal system. Feedback is the most precious resource any service provider can have. Feedback helps agencies to understand the public sentiments, about services and functioning of the system. Feedback can be gathered in a variety of ways:

A suggestion box: The most direct way of getting feedback, of course, is at the point of contact. Every citizen must have the opportunity to tell you what he/she thinks and a suggestion box is the simplest way. Make sure there is writing material near the box.

A small questionnaire: A brief questionnaire asking the citizen to fill out what they came in for, whether their visit was fruitful and how long it took for their needs to be catered to, etc. This would go a long way in assessing how your 'front-office' staff is doing for customer-friendliness.

Follow-up: A follow-up telephone call to make sure that the customer is happy with services or products creates a lot of good will for your department. E-seva followed up service with a survey and found that their service actually yielded desired results.

Mailed questionnaires: These are useful for slightly long-term feedback, to see how you've performed over three or six months.

Customer contact: Senior officers must interact often with customers to assess what their needs are and if your department is meeting them to satisfaction. Tata Telecom, for example, asked their senior managers to sit in the service counters and interact with customers. As a result, the feedback they got proved invaluable.

Customer surveys: A survey—either a formal one through an external agency, or one conducted by your own department staff—can tell you much about what your customers think of your services, what else they need and the ways in which you can improve. For instance, Vijayawada Municipal Corporation surveyed its residents and found it to be an excellent source of information to improve services.

Focus groups: Meeting consumer organisations also reveals much about expectations from your department. LIC recently held meetings with consumer organisations to find out issues of policy holders and realised that there was a need to introduce new products and services.

Multiple channels of communication: The citizen must be able to contact your department through various channels: through telephone, post, e-mail, fax, the Internet and in person. All numbers and addresses must be well publicised, so your customer has no trouble reaching you. For instance, reacting to a series of burglaries, Karkhana Police in 2004-05 issued stickers containing a list of emergency contact numbers to every house in the area. The initiative raised a feeling of security in the area and was very well received by the local community.

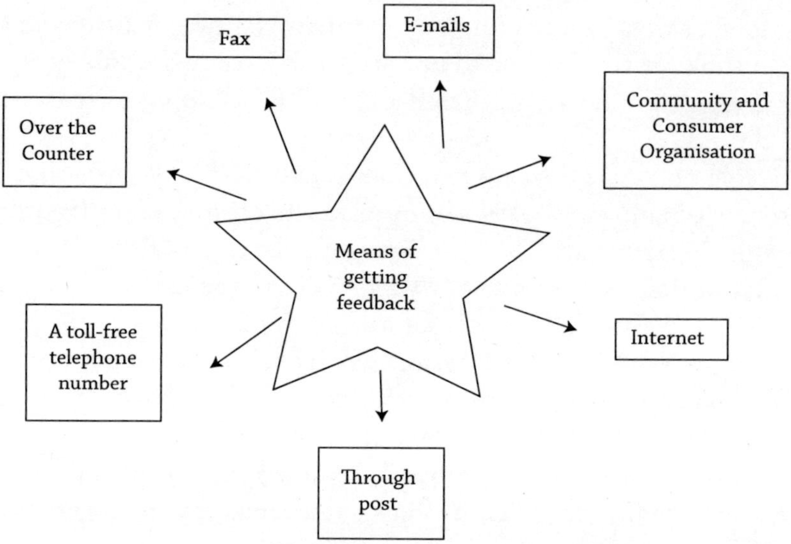

Publishing Complaints Information: Publishing complaints information is in line with the principle of general public service accountability and transparency. The action demonstrates to the public that complaints are taken seriously and it is worthwhile to complain. The department must publish information on complaints received at least on a yearly basis and should include:

- Numbers and types/categories of complaints;
- Speed of response to the complaints received;
- Action taken as a result of complaints to improve services.

Organisations must decide for themselves the level of detail to be recorded about complaints received, but minimum data should include:

- Name, address and telephone number of the complainant.
- Date of receipt.
- Details of the complaint, subject/issue.
- What redress the person wants.
- Immediate action to be taken on the complaint.

Information about complaints should be submitted to the senior officers and policy makers on a regular basis.

Use Information Technology (IT) Tools

IT has given an added feature to the way in which information can be stored in government departments. The data on complaints are stored with ease and can be accessed comfortably without tedious record maintenance. The database becomes accessible to every level of the administration and redress is also possible more effectively and quickly; it becomes convenient to record and track complaints and produce reports on complaint redressal. This also enables measurement of customer satisfaction through analysis of questionnaires generated amongst users.

Changing Attitudes: If a complaint system is to be effective, simply having procedures may not be enough. It is important that staff have the 'right attitude' towards complaints. This involves:

- Listening sympathetically to people who have felt a cause to complain;
- Recognising that complaints handling is an integral part both of good service and customer care and not a nuisance.
- Understanding the benefits of good complaints handling and consequences of poor complaints handling and welcome complaints as an opportunity.
- Putting things right for the citizen and to learn the lesson and improve service.

In the same context, the eight step Gift Formula devised by Janelle Barlow and Claus Moller is extremely useful. The Gift Formula is a step-by-step process that, in its optimal form, is delivered in a set order. Having said this, there might be occasions when it will be more appropriate to vary the sequence. The steps are as follows:

Say 'Thank you': Do not think about whether customers have a legitimate complaint or not. Just consider the complaint valuable information and thank them for the gift. The expression should be as natural and spontaneous as the gratitude shown when receiving a gift/present. It must be made sure that the body language demonstrates appreciation for the complaint and that the service provider supports the customer's right to complain. Eye contact, an understanding nod, and a friendly smile can work wonders.

Explain why you appreciate the complaint: 'Thank you' by itself can sound empty. You need to qualify it by saying something about how hearing the complaint will allow you to better address the problem.

Apologise for the mistake: It is important to apologise to customers, but it should not be the first step. You create a more powerful rapport with customers by saying, "Thank you, I appreciate your telling me about this." This is then followed by the apology.

Promise to do something about the problem immediately. Once you have apologised, do not ask for anything else right away. Do not start to interview the customer. Service recovery has two aspects: psychological and tangible. The psychological dimension helps everyone feel better about the situation that has created dissatisfaction. The tangible dimension is doing something to fix the situation. Tangible responses are steps that will cost money or time. Steps one through four of the Gift Formula are part of the psychological response; they cost nothing and are easy to implement.

Ask for necessary information: "In order for me to give you fast service, could you please give me some information?" Do not say, "I need some information, otherwise I can't help you," you are the one asking for help from the customers. They are the ones who have brought you the gift. Ask only for what is necessary. But ask for all relevant details as by questioning, you will discover the real problem. Sometimes they only want to let you know something happened and don't necessarily want anything from you.

Correct the mistake—promptly: Do what you said you would do. A sense of urgency will be greatly appreciated by the customer. Rapid responses say you are serious about service recovery. A sense of urgency lets you get back in balance with the customer. The Gift Formula will not be adequate if you do not fix the problems to the customer's satisfaction.

Check customer satisfaction—follow up: Call your customers back to find out what happened. Ask them directly if they are satisfied with what you did for them. If appropriate, tell them what you are doing to prevent this from happening in the future so that they feel good about having helped you with their complaints. Thank them again for your complaints. You are now in partnership.

Prevent future mistakes. Make the complaint known throughout the organisation so that this kind of problem can be prevented in the future. Fix the system without rushing to blame the staff. Punish your processes, not your people. Staff members will be more likely to pass along complaints to management if they know this is the company's approach to complaints.

Complaints systems are unlikely to be fully effective if they are not supported and supervised at higher levels. Senior officials should regularly review complaints information and ensure that complaints handling is built into all performance reports of the department. Each department may consider putting up on a display board their PLEDGE to welcome complaints.

Grievance Handling and Right to Information Act 2005

Right to Information (RTI) Act can be used as a tool to check the efficiency of a grievance handling system. In the light of the fact that every grievance, handling mechanism will have an official functionary in charge of handling complaints, the RTI Act through its provisions automatically places a large responsibility on the functionary to carry out his/her duties with more diligence and transparency.

Every piece of information can be brought under the act's purview. As a matter of right, a citizen can demand any information with regard to the working of a grievance management cell/department established in any public authority, and for the purpose of this module, in a local self-governing institution. The stipulations of the act require that the information sought will need to be furnished within 30 days from date of application (40 days if third party is involved) and within 48 hours in cases of information related to life and liberty.

1) What specific information relating to grievances handling in particular falls out of the purview of the RTI Act?
    - Information that would prejudicially affect the sovereignty, integrity, security, scientific or economic interest and relation with a foreign state.

- Information received in confidence from a foreign government.
- Information which would lead to commission of an offence.
- If it is likely to impede investigation and prosecution processes.
- If it is about a source of information or assistance given in confidence of law enforcement or security purposes.
- Cabinet papers including deliberations of council of ministers, secretaries and other officers.
- Information whose release is forbidden by a court or tribunal or disclosure which might constitute contempt of court.
- Personal or private information subject to larger public interest to be decided by the public information officer.
- Commercial and trade secrets, intellectual property, etc., that would harm competitive position of third party subject to public interest to be decided by competent authority.
- Information available to a person in his fiduciary relationship subject to public interest to be decided by the competent authority.

2) How does the RTI Act provide an impetus to making a Grievance Redressal System more effective?

- Although efficiency in the private sector may be judged in solely economic terms, it cannot be so simply evaluated in the public sphere of government.
- Service efficiency is manifested in the effective provision of services to the public, responsive to public opinion and so on. Thus, the efficiency in government must be measured in terms of all three facets of efficiency. The requirements of the act place heavy emphasis on each of these also. Literally every step taken can be questioned

making the act an intrinsic self-correcting mechanism and thereby helping a grievance redressal system become more efficient.

Some tips for prompt and effective redress of grievances:

- Grievances should be necessarily acknowledged, with an interim reply within 3 days of receipt and redressed within 3 months of receipt in the organisation. The same time limit should apply even if co-ordination with subsidiary offices or another department/organisation is involved. In such instances special efforts, to be *suo moto* disclosed when reports are called, should be made.
- No grievance is to be rejected without having been independently examined.

  At a minimum, this means that a superior officer, to the one who delayed taking the original decision or took the original decision that is cause for grievance, should actually examine the case as well as the reply, intended to be sent to the grievance holder.

  Make the 'Director of Grievances' effective through the following inter-related steps:
- Secretaries/organisational heads or the highest officer at the local body level should ensure that Directors of Grievances so appointed in that body are fully 'empowered' in accordance with instructions to perform their role.
- All grievance representations received in the department/Organisation, either by mail, fax, and e-mail to be invariably routed through Director of Grievances before they go to concerned sections/divisions. At this stage, Office of the Director of Grievances shall go through the representations and come to a *prima facie* view regarding the gravity of the matter involved and decide whether it shall monitor the case or allow down-the-line functionaries to independently deal with it. Directors of Grievances should monitor and follow up at least 3 to 5

per cent of grievances received to enable them to assess the efficacy of grievance redress mechanism.

- Fix responsibility in each case of delay, default and dereliction of duty, identified by Director of Grievances, and take appropriate action against concerned personnel. In addition, consider feasibility of prescribing specific penalty clauses for such failures.

Points to Remember

- Listen to the customer and acknowledge his or her complaint. People don't usually register complaints with only a casual interest. Complaining involves some inconvenience and possibly expense.
- Do not take problems and complaints personally. Do not get defensive when people complain, and do not jump to conclusions about their causes or solutions.
- Show concern for the customer. Personalise the response. If the customer is angry, use calming positive sentences.
- Ask questions to identify and analyse the problem.
- Find out whether the person actually seeks any action from you or whether they just want to let you know.
- Decide fairly what you or your department is responsible for and initiate some positive action to remedy the situation. Make sure that the customer knows that the problem has been recorded.
- Follow through with the proposed resolution. If it can't be resolved immediately, keep the customer informed of progress. Make a note of the promised action.
- Thank the person for reporting the problem: it's better you know about it than you don't.

Many central and state governments adopted grievance redressal mechanism and they designed it in their own style. In fact, most of the government's experiments were fairly simple, but effective strategies to bring in transparency and responsiveness in the functioning of government departments through and effective use of information technology applications. The model of Lokvani in Sitapur District of Uttar Pradesh was a best practice. Government of Andhra Pradesh was one of the few states to design an online grievance redressal mechanism for public service delivery departments. The web-based application is a generic application for all the departments which captures the service request of each department and the time frame in which the services are redressed. This application serves as an effective monitoring mechanism to the citizens, as well as the higher officials in the departments and can be used to detect the bottle necks in the process of redressing the requests. There are several reports that can be generated through this application which the responsiveness of the departments can be measured. These reports can be used to monitor the performance of the department officials and they can be given incentives or disincentives, also can be linked to the Performance Monitoring System. The model was replicated in a big way in some of the central governments and state governments. We will discuss some best practices in the next chapter.

References

Griglani, C. (2006). *A Report on Grievance Redressal System in Government*, submitted to DFID, Institute of Public Enterprise, Hyderabad.

5

Best Practices in Citizen's Charter Implementation

Government of India (GoI), in 1997, launched the citizen's charter programme based on the UK model. Many states implemented the charter programme and even made tremendous progress in the initial years of implementation. States like Andhra Pradesh (AP), Gujarat, Karnataka, Madhya Pradesh (MP) and many others made considerable progress in implementation of citizen's charters. Government of Kerala even provided a legal backing to citizen's charter by making it mandatory for all the local self-government institutions to implement charters through the Panchayat Act. In this chapter, we will talk about some best practices which are well known and try to narrate some of the interesting experiments done by various state governments.

The Andhra Pradesh Experience

The citizen's charter process in AP started initially in the year 1998 with an orientation for the ministers, secretaries and senior officers of the state government. The government identified seven key departments which has high public interface, initially, for focused implementation of charters. These departments were Municipal Corporation of Hyderabad (MCH), Andhra Pradesh Road Transport Authority, Andhra Pradesh Transco, Hyderabad Metro Works and Sewerage and Sanitation Board (Parigi and Geeta, 2002).

The Andhra Pradesh Road Transport Authority took up the extensive process of reengineering and used IT (information technology) in the implementation process. The organisation also involved the internal staff in the process of change and also the civil society for greater acceptability to change. The key factor that led to the success of the organisation was the total support from the government. There were extensive consultations held with all stakeholders from time to time during the process reengineering phase. The process is an ongoing one and the organisation is still exploring the possibility of reducing timelines for service delivery on some of the services like issue of licences etc., by use of IT. The process is continuing in Road Transport Authority (RTA) for providing services faster to the common man. Information and grievance redressal mechanism is in place wherein a toll free (1074) facility for disseminating information regarding services/complaints is available. All information pertaining to citizen services and forms are available through web on *www.aptransport.org/www.aptransport.gov.in* and feedback forms are monitored for betterment. The system has resulted in greater transparency, accountability and increased efficiency of the staff. The revenues have also increased through effective monitoring and effective check on circulation of bogus licences/registrations/ permits.

The Greater Hyderabad Municipal Corporation (GHMC) is another department which took a big step towards accessibility, transparency and accountability through the use of e-governance. The approach the organisation has chosen to take towards e-governance is to make it a paperless organisation with authenticated and accurate digital data. Adherence to the citizen's charters is made mandatory to bring in greater transparency and accountability. As a part of the 'Hyderabad First' project that reaches out to the citizens, the following services are offered:

- Settlement and payment of Property Tax.
- Payment Gateway for Online Payments.
- Digital Signatures.
- Instant Birth/Death Registration.
- Instant Birth/Death Certificates' Issuance.
- ILook.
- C2C Services.
- Fund Your City.

- Submission and tracking of Building Plan Applications.
- Public Grievance lodging through Parishkruthi.
- Tenders' Submission and Management System.
- File Management System.
- Legal Case Management System.
- Citizens Forum.
- Opinion Polls and Geographic Information System (GIS) for resource planning and decision-making.
- City Managers' Training Centre.
- AASARA for Senior Citizens.
- Status of Infrastructure Works.

Online Issue of Birth and Death Certificates

Another major feature of the programme is that citizens can get their birth/death certificates delivered to them quickly. Citizens have the facility to indent these certificates through the website which is sent through courier to their door steps. By maintaining the database of births and deaths on the computer, the process of sorting, searching and accessing the database is now simplified. The citizens can get their records updated, as they have the facility of checking whether their name is registered or not, through the website. The Citizen Service Centres or e-Seva centres provide the citizens the facility to collect their certificates on demand instantly. This is made possible because the records pertaining to them have been thrown open and it is now possible for them to get necessary rectification on their records without any delay.

An Integrated eGovernance Programme in Andhra Pradesh: Mee Seva Experiment

The National e-Governance Plan (NeGP) formulated by GoI, visualises that all basic services required by a common man will be delivered at his/her doorstep at an affordable cost. It provides an overarching framework for e-Governance initiatives in the country by bringing in convergence among various initiatives across departments and maximising benefits to the citizen (Geeta, 2007). Basing on these ideas, massive initiatives have been taken up across the country to build basic infrastructure to reach remotest villages, computerisation of records in key service delivery departments to enable easy, reliable access over the internet. According to the Vision Statement of NeGP, the ultimate objective is to bring public services closer home to citizens. The institutional mechanism suggested by the government for implementation of this mega plan is to set up service delivery points at the costumer service centres as the front end or the first point contact of the government, formation of district e-governance societies under the chairmanship of district collector to coordinate and implement e-district, state wide area network (SWAN), citizen service centre (CSC), and other e-governance initiatives at the district level. Thus, enabling an environment for improved service delivery to the common man has been created and initiated in our country.

In sync with the country-wide initiatives being taken up on e-governance front, Government of Andhra Pradesh (GoAP) initiated the process of simplifying services to the citizens and bringing about greater transparency and accountability in public service delivery. The GoAP has already set up in place APSWAN, AP State Data Centre, e-Seva Centres, APonline Centres, and Common Service Centres in sync with the plan. A major step was taken by the government to knit all these initiatives together to harness the benefits of the above for the rural citizens. Government initiated work on providing for a reliable and secured architecture for delivering various citizen services with data securely hosted in the State Data Centre (SDC), to be used by each of the state designated agencies providing services through CSCs.[1] Thus, the Mee Seva project was conceived and launched by the Hon'ble Chief Minister of Andhra Pradesh Sri Kiran Kumar Reddy in Chittoor district on 4 November 2011. A lot of preparatory work was done prior to the launch of this project. One of the major steps prior to launching the Mee Seva project was that the government brought out rules called Andhra Pradesh Information Technology (Electronic Service Delivery; ESD) Rules, 2011

1. National eGovernance Plan Overview, NeGP Round Table, New Delhi, 29 July 2009.

vide G.O.Ms.10, IT&C Department, dated 18 October 2011 (GoAP, 2011). The key features are as follows:

- Use of Digital Certificates: The ESD rules 2011 provides for enabling and regulating the filling of forms of applications and for the issue of grant of digitally signed licences, permits, certificates, sanctions or approvals and the receipt or payment of money for the delivery of services electronically to the users.
- Delivery of Services through Electronic Mode: The government departments are directed to publish, within 180 days, the various services they would provide through electronic mode and the timelines within which it would be done including service standards to be prescribed. It also directs departments to identify nodal officers responsible for the above initiatives. The maximum timeline granted for departments to switch over to the electronic mode of service delivery is within next five years.
- Institutional Mechanism for Electronic Service Delivery: The Director, EDS (e-Seva), has been designated as Director of Electronic Service Delivery as per the act to oversee the entire operations of electronic service delivery by departments. Authorising service providers, ensuring accountable and efficient service delivery and entire responsibility of supervision are vested with the Director.

  At the district level, a Special Deputy Collector has been designated to ensure smooth implementation, better coordination and review with the participating departments like the concerned revenue authorities, municipalities, offices of electricity distribution companies and any other department whose services are being offered through Mee Seva. The district heads are also responsible for ensuring readiness of departmental databases, digitally signing them and installing the requisite hardware and software. The other major responsibility of Special Deputy Collectors is to redressal of customer grievances and smooth functioning of services.[2]

---

2. Information Technology and Communications Department, G.O.Rt. No.1, dated 01 January 2012.

Each district has been provided with one resource person reporting to the Joint Collector/Additional Director, ESD, to give hand holding support to the concerned officers in the district. The centres delivering Mee Seva services have been advised by the state government to have a common look and feel across the states including aspects such as colour scheme, display boards, citizen's charters boards, notice boards, etc.

- Penalty: The key feature of the rules is provision for penalty for committing fraud knowingly or unknowingly or misinterpreting facts.
- Implementation Aspect: As a part preparatory work, the Information Technology and Communication (IT&C) Department, which is the lead department in the implementation of the project held consultative meetings with supply side stakeholders from Revenue Department, Registration Department, District Heads, technical support organisations like National Information Centre (NIC), AP-Online and others.

The salient feature of this project is that there is a centralised database which ensures uniformity, data security, integrity and reliability. These data can be accessed by various stakeholders through the SWAN. The other key feature is digital signatures; manual methods have been completely kept aside in the implementation of this project.

As a part of the plan, the Service Delivery Points should have a standardised look and feel with display boards, posters, common facilities, etc. Responsibility for monitoring the field operations has been given to the service centre agency and the village level entrepreneur. However a one-time lump sum monetary incentive can be given to the VLEs of the Pilot Districts adhering to the above guidelines. The project envisages incentivising especially the rural Mee Seva centres (CSCs/APOnline) in pilot districts with ₹10,000 where the centres adhere to the infrastructure norms and guidelines indicated by the government.[3]

---

3. Government of Andhra Pradesh, Information Technology and Communications Department. G.O.Ms.No 4, dated 1 March 2012, Lr. No. 05/Mee Seva/Secy/IT&C/2012, dated 5 March 2012.

Services Included

The project works on an Integrated Service Delivery Model to provide a single entry point for a wide range of services to the citizens, "easier and faster" (Institute of Public Enterprise, 2012-13). The project provides different types of services which come under Revenue Department, Health Department, Registration Department, School Department and GHMC. These services are categorised as Category 'A' services and Category 'B' services as indicated below:

Category A

- These are the services to be given across the counter from e-Seva or by the Kiosk operator.
- No supporting documents required to be given at the Kiosk.

Category B

- Transaction/statutory in nature
- Notices/hearings/field inspections required.

The procedure for processing requests under Category 'A' Services has been outlined by the government in the Department User Manual:

- All the digitally signed databases stored in the SECR.
- Citizen comes to CSC for submission of application of certificates.
- Applicant purchases and fills up a physical application form.
- CSC operator enters the details online and issues the digitally signed paper.
- A receipt of acknowledgement is also given to the applicant.

The procedure for processing requests under Category 'B' services has also been outlined by the government in the Department User Manual:

Category 'B1'

- Citizen comes to the CSC and fills up the physical application form.
- Applicant purchases and fills up the form.

- CSC operator enters the details in the online application software and issues a receipt to the applicant.
- In this case, there may be a need to submit supporting documents as per the checklist. This formality of physical transfer of the paper documents can in due course be digitised by adding a scanner and providing uploads in the application.
- *Tahasildars* log into their online portal to download the applications and verify the records.
- If the record is not available already, due process is followed for generating the record and are then digitally signed and uploaded.

Category 'B2'

- Citizen comes to the CSC and fills up the physical application form.
- Applicant purchases and fills up the form.
- CSC operator enters the details in the Online Application Software and issues a receipt to the applicant.
- If there is a need to submit supporting documents as per the checklist, this formality of physical transfer of the paper documents can in due course be digitised by adding a scanner and providing uploads in the application.
- *Tahasildars* log into their online portal to download the applications and verify the records.
- Applicant has to appear on the date of enquiry on the field along with relevant documents.
- *Tahasildars* approve or reject, based on the fields of the verification report.
- If the record is not available already, due process is followed for generating the record and digitally signed and uploaded.
- If the record is available in physical form, *Tahasildar* signs, scans and uploads it on the portal.

All the digitally signed certificates are kept stored in the State Electronic Certificate Repository (SECR). The Kiosk then takes printouts of the certificates and they are delivered to the address of the applicant; also details of delivery are sent by SMS (short service message) to the applicant. In case, the application is rejected, *Tahasildar* has to enter the reasons for rejection. As indicated in the Mee Seva portal, the total number of requests received through Mee Seva till 10 November 2012 is as follows:

Total Requests :	66,72,755
Cat A :	22,36,293
Cat B :	44,36,462
Total Approved :	38,51,237
Total Rejected :	2,48,401
Pending within SLA :	3,02,215
Pending beyond SLA :	34,606

The Gujarat Experience

The Ahmedabad district in Gujarat experimented with a public grievance redressal mechanism coupled with e-governance in 1998. The district authorities realised that the traditional redressal mechanisms suffered from lacunae and the grievance redressal process was riddled with problems such as inadequate information, delivering services beyond time limits, no acknowledgement of applications and a general culture of apathy on the part of the government functionaries responsible for the delivery of public services. With this background, the Government of Gujarat vide its resolution dated 8 October 1998 adopted the formulation and implementation of the Citizen's Charters in government functioning (Karwal, 2004). The District Collectorate of Ahmedabad published its citizen's charter in the local language which consisted of 75 items covering the entire gamut of functioning of the Collectorate of Ahmedabad. The government also adopted a single window approach by introducing Citizens' Facilitation Centres to be set up across the state. These centres were supposed to acknowledge receipt of applications/grievances, inform the citizen of the time limit for disposal, keep a track of the computerised management information system (MIS) and send the application to the concerned office for further action within time limit.

Despite these initiatives, there was no effective implementation of citizen's charters in the district and reasons were de-motivated staff, poor infrastructure of service provider, archaic processes and procedures, etc. The government adopted a two-pronged strategy to deal with the situation. The first decision was to improve the infrastructure and shift office to another premise and to combine the citizen's charter with an e-governance initiative. Jan Sewa Kendras (citizen facilitation centres) were set up in the districts' and talukas' head quarters to ensure maximum accessibility for information regarding each and every service in the citizen's charter and its procedures by publicising through a website, brochures, and booklets. Standardised and user-friendly formats for each item of the citizen's charter were made available at the Jan Sewa Kendras along with making the formats available for downloading from the websites.

The standardised formats gave brief and user-friendly information on the following:

- Provisions of law related to the issue.
- Office/officer authorised to take final decision.
- Maximum time limit for disposal.
- Maximum time limit to be taken at each level of hierarchy.

Jan Sewa Kendras also provide information regarding status of citizen's applications. This information was also made available on the daily updated screens on the website. This gave an opportunity for the citizens to track their application and interact with the authorities to prevent delay. Time limits and other details were notified through display boards at the Jan Sewa Kendras for disposal of cases. Adequate publicity was made to provide enough publicity regarding the location and working hours of Jan Sewa Kendras. Special facilities such as drinking water, toilets, ramps for the physically challenged, stamp franking facility, banking facility for depositing government dues, a clean environment, etc., were also made available to the citizens at the *kendras*.

The district administration took up a huge task of re-engineering the internal processes to make them smooth, speedy and user-friendly. Capacity building, programmes and initiatives to tackle the mindset changes of service provider were also attempted strongly. Need assessment exercises was carried out by outside experts along with the collector to understand the infrastructure needs (including software and hardware requirements) and capacity building needs of staff and employees. Consultations were held with employees, citizens (both urban and rural), industry, ICT partners, people's representatives and higher officials. It was clear that there was need to change employee mindset, bring change in work environment by moving into an office location with all facilities and ambience, process reengineering, fixing standards, fixing user responsibilities and using technology. The Jan Sewa Kendra office had a clean, green and inviting environment, and these offices were extended to each *taluka* head quarters. For all these above initiatives, the finances were not provided by the state government. Finances were sought from non-governmental sources such as banks, cooperative societies and industrial houses on a public-private partnership model that utilised the idea of 'corporate social responsibility,' community involvement and partnerships in order to scale-up and deliver better quality services.

As a part of the process of re-engineering, the government initiated computerisation of the following services in back office as well as front office.

- Ration card (issue of new cards online)
- Employee's personal information system, human resource (HR), payrolls, pension, General Provident Fund (GPF), etc.
- Old age pension scheme.
- Collection and monitoring of land revenue.
- Collection and monitoring of luxury tax and entertainment tax.
- Land records (expansion).
- Registration (i.e., sub-registrar's office).
- Legal case system

- MP, MLA grants—District Planning Board.
- Record Management.
- Dead Stock Management.

In order to make the government rely on IT and not on paper, the following governmental activities were also computerised:

- Alien Recovery.
- Accounts and Budgeting.
- Land Resource Management.
- Land Acquisition.
- Planning for infrastructure development (tourism, industry, etc.).
- Database for scarcity relief, floods and other disasters.
- Disbursement of government relief in natural and man-made disasters.
- Government orders and amendments.
- Registration (i.e., sub-registrar's office).
- Monitoring of various other government schemes.
- Publishing the electoral roll in the public domain.

Fixing Delivery Standards

As a part of the process of re-engineering procedures, an interesting exercise was done to trace the movement of application related to each service identified in the citizen's charter. It was found out that in most cases, the number of tables through which an application moved was much larger, sometimes double the number of the days notified for disposal. For all other applications, the minimum number of tables through which each moved was 65. Therefore, to meet the time limits declared in the citizen's charter, process of re-engineering was undertaken by the government functionaries themselves. They were made to identify scope for level jumping, deletion of obsolete procedures and number of days that each of these applications could spend for processing in various levels of the hierarchy.

Based on the process of re-engineering initiatives in the new revised procedure, the number of tables through which each application related to the services indicated in the citizen's charter moves ranged from 5 to 30. In the new system, the applicant was required to provide a completed application as incomplete applications were not accepted, thus ensuring that papers do not pass to and fro between the citizen's and government offices. One of the main reasons which prompted this decision to combine the citizen's charter programme with an e-governance initiative was a study of the applications received under the citizen's charter since its formulation in 1998 as shown below:

S.No.	*Time Period*	*No. of Applications*
1	December 1998 to December 1999	987
2	January 2000 to December 2000	48993
3	January 2001 to December 2001	45107
4.	January 2002 to December 2002	79616
5.	January 2003 to December 2003	132792
6	February 2004 to November 2004	90927

The employees were under tremendous pressure to dispose of these applications within the stipulated time period. A detailed analysis showed that more than 80 per cent of the applications in any given year were related to the following issues of the citizen's charter:

S.No.	*Citizen's Charters Issues*	*Actual Time Taken for Disposal (Pre-Jan Sewa Kendra)*	*Time Limit Fixed for Disposal (Days) (Pre-Jan Sewa Kendra)*	*Time Limit Fixed in Jan Sewa Kendra*
1	Addition/deletion/ modification of name in the ration card	5	2	1
2	Issue of Income certificate	25	10	1
3	Issue of language/religious minority certificate	7	2	1
4	Certificate for socially and educationally backward class	10	5	1
5.	Certificate for caste	14	7	1
6.	Certificate for proof of residence	14	7	1
7.	Domicile certificate	30	7	1

In the new system, processes were re-engineered and systems smoothened to ensure that all the above issues were brought under the same day disposal process i.e., a time limit of only one day. Both the system and the citizens stood to benefit. Later, when the Jan Sewa Kendra was inaugurated and started functioning on 9 February 2004, it was pandemonium for 3-4 days. Almost all the Class I officers including collector had to literally direct its functioning all through the day. This experience led our partners Microtech System Company to hire a retired and experienced Deputy Mamlatdar to co-ordinate the activities of the Jan Sewa Kendra. The initial problem of excessive demand for service at the Jan Sewa Kendra outstripping the supply had to be resolved by increasing the number of terminals from 8 to 16 within 15 days of starting the kendra.

User charge for ₹20 per application was introduced in the *kendras*. While 70 per cent of the user charges go towards the cost of the recovery of the software and the establishment cost of the data entry operators, stationery, ink and maintenance of the hardware by the private partners, rest of the 30 per cent is utilised by the Collectorate to expand its e-governance net down to the block headquarters and also ensure continuous improvement in the system. Employee skill upgradation and simultaneous back office automation have ensured smooth follow-up. The initiative is in place in all the taluka headquarters. One of the most important lessons learned in the project is that to sustain change, the service providers must own the entire change process. In our system of bureaucracy, it is difficult to ensure continuity at the top management/leadership levels. Therefore, it is essential that the leaders push from behind rather than lead from the front. It is imperative that once the system is devised there must be formal written procedures, understood and followed by all employees. Also the know-how of the systems and processes in toto must be available with several of the employees rather than just a handful of them. In the Ahmedabad initiative, along with the process of re-engineering, software development and capacity building in the work place environment for the employees underwent a sea change too. With the written support of the state government, through private partnership and active participation of the employees, the new office was made clean, green and airy, with employee friendly infrastructure.

Citizen's Charter

S.No.	*Subject*	*Time Limit for Disposal in Days*
1.	Assignment of Land for village site	75
2.	Application for Land from Govt. Departments under Administrative Order–3	40
3.	Application for Govt. Land for Non-Agriculture Purpose/ by Registered Organisation/ Co-operative Society	120
4.	Application for Govt. Land for the Purpose of Agriculture by Cooperative Societies.	90
5.	Application for Gaucher Land for Gram Van Project (Social Forestry)	65
6.	Application for Land for Fisheries/Prawn Farming	90
7.	Applications for Govt. Land for the purpose of Agriculture through Land Kacheri (for individual)	120
8.	Application for Govt. Land for the purpose of Non-Agriculture (for individual)	120
9.	Application for Govt. Land for the purpose of Non-Agriculture (Govt. Servant)	120
10.	Application for Govt. Land for the purpose of Non-Agriculture (Govt. Servant)	120
11.	Application for Govt. Land for the Purpose of Non-Agriculture (for Ex.Serviceman)	120
12.	Application for Govt. Land (of Road/ City Survey Area) by Sale/Lease (Only for Nagarpalika/Nagar Panchayat Area	120
13.	Assigning Land for Crematorium/Cemetery Ground	90
14.	Application for Land for Salt Industries on lease	120
15.	Regularisation of Gamtaal/Simtaal vada Land Regulation.	120
16.	Permission for Cutting Trees (Panchayat Area)	25
17.	Permission for Cutting Trees (Private Ownership Area)	15
18.	Non-Agriculture Permission use Under Land Revenue Code 65	90
19.	Removal of the Restriction of Prohibited Tenure for Agriculture use	60
20.	Removal of the Restriction of new Tenure for Agriculture use	60

contd...

contd...

21.	Permission under Tenancy Act. Sec. 63 for sale to a Non-Agriculturist for N.A. use.	90
22.	Permission under the Tenancy Act Sec. 63 AA	90
23.	Permission under the Tenancy Act. Sec. 43 for the Transfer of Land for Agricultural Purpose.	90
24.	Permission under the Tenancy Act. Sec. 43 for the Transfer of land for Non-Agricultural Purpose.	90
25.	Permission of Block Division under Fragmentation & Consolidation Act.	45
26.	Certificate under the L.R Code 65-B (New Industrial Policy	90
27.	Permission for consolidation of Land for Agricultural Purpose	15
28.	Certificate for Agriculturist	15
29.	Certificate of Small Farmer	15
30.	License of Stamp Vendor	60
31.	Renewal of Stamp Vendor's License	15
32.	Death Relief in Natural Calamity (Urban Areas)	7
33.	Grant of Agency of small Savings Schemes (For N.S.C./ K.V.P./M.I.S Scheme)	15
34.	Grant of Agency of Mahila Pradhan Kshetriya Bachat Scheme (Recurring Deposit)	15
35.	Issue of Solvency Certificate	25
36.	Issue of O.B.C. Certificate	7
37.	Certified Copies	15
38.	Old Age & Handicapped Pension Scheme	60
39.	Financial Assistance under the National Family Benefit Scheme (Only for Nagarpalika Area)	45
40.	Relief for Solarium Fund (Hit and Run Cases)	60
41.	Certificate of Succession the case of death of pensioners	20
42.	Renewal of Arms License for Self protection	15
43.	License for booking premises	45
44.	Storage license under Explosives Act	90
45.	Fresh Arms License for Self-protection	75
46.	Duplicate license under Explosive Act	90
47.	License for Manufacturing of Permissible Explosive	60

contd...

contd...

48.	Permanent license for sale of permissible explosive	3
49.	Temporary license for sale of permissible explosive	21
50.	Renewal of explosive license	15
51.	Storage license under the petroleum storage act	120
52.	Poison license	120
53.	Hotel License	45
54.	Renewal of Hotel license	15
55.	Issue of Video License	30
56.	Dish antenna License	14
57.	Issue of New Ration Card	30
58.	Issue of Separate Ration Card	30
59.	Issue of Duplicate Ration Card	7
60.	Addition/deletion/modification of name in the ration card	2
61.	Issue of Agency Card	30
62.	License of retails/wholesaler & manufacturer	45
63.	Change of name/address/location in the license	30
64.	Change of partner in retailer/wholesaler/manufacturer and petroleum	30
65.	Sanction of new fair price shop	120
66.	Issue of permit for kerosene to organisation	30
67.	License for solvent	45
68.	Issue of free sale kerosene registration certificate	30
69.	Issue of income certificate.	1
70.	Issue of certificate for persons from Language/Religious Minority Group.	1
71.	Certificate for Socially and Educationally backward class	1
72.	Certificate for S.C./S.T.	1
73.	Certificate of Residential Proof	1
74.	Certificate of Domicile	1
75.	Widow Certificate	1

References

Parigi, V.K. and P. Geeta (2002). *A Guide to Developing and Implementing Citizen's Charter.* Centre for Good Governance, Government of Andhra Pradesh.

Geeta, P. (2007). *A Brief on the Training on Citizen's Charters and Social Accountability for the Participants of CESSD Project.* Government of Pakistan Centre for Good Governance, Hyderabad.

Government of Andhra Pradesh (2011). *Andhra Pradesh Information Technology (Electronic Service Delivery) Rules.* Information Technology and Communications Department.

Institute of Public Enterprise (2012-13). *An Assessment Report on Mee Seva.* Information Technology and Communications Department, Government of Andhra Pradesh.

Karwal, Anita (2004). *eGovernance Initiatives for Improving District Collecorate.* Paper presented at a training programme at HIPA, Rajasthan.

6

Best Practices in Grievance Redressal Mechanism

A number of states in India appreciated the need for a robust Grievance Redressal Mechanism (GRM) and many of them even implemented it with varying degrees of success. GRM was packaged forming under the citizen's charter process and therefore, it was under the charter initiative that a GRM was set up. In this chapter, we will discuss some of the early initiatives taken by the state governments.

The Andhra Pradesh Experience

One of the earliest initiatives of setting up a grievance redressal mechanism was in the Vizianagaram District of Andhra Pradesh in the year 2003 (Centre for Good Governance [CGG], 2004). It was a web-based grievance monitoring system. The District Collector felt that petitions filed by citizens was being substantially delayed due to the physical movement of files from one department to another, and in some cases the original petitions were also lost. It was also learnt that people travelled hundreds of miles only to know the status of their petition, which resulted in loss of their valuable time and money. Most of them were villagers and very poor people, who couldn't afford to travel frequently. So, the Collector felt the need to have a web-based monitoring system for tracking of the petitions for various departments. Through this system, the Collector of Vizianagaram received about 200-300 petitions every week from citizens of the district. This tool effectively helped in reducing the time involved in transferring of files, because the files were being transferred electronically, thus eliminating the chances of losing the petitions in transit. This also helped the departments to redress the petitions within the time frame. The collector monitored the responsiveness of the departments through the reports provided by the system. The tool generated comparative graphs for the redressal of petitions by various departments.

Parishkaram: Call Centre Application

To help the farmers get the right information on farming-related issues and to facilitate discussions with officials from agriculture department, Parishkaram—a call centre for farmers—was launched on 1 July 2003 by the Government of Andhra Pradesh (GoAP) (Geeta, 2007). This call centre is meant to be a single source of information pertaining to all agricultural issues from which the farmer could get information with a single toll free phone call numbered '1111' from his place and from anywhere in the state. The call centre consists of scientists from Acharaya N.G. Ranga Agricutural University (ANGRAU) dealing with different divisions and experienced officials from agriculture department who deliver information to all the needful farmers in achieving best results. Before this facility was made available, due to their ignorance and illiteracy, the farmers blindly followed age old agricultural techniques irrespective of season and used less branded grains which resulted in less and unfruitful product. But now, the farmers directly call the call centre to clarify their doubts and get required information. The strategy adopted by the government was very simple and effective, apart from providing the best possible solution to the farmer with regard to his/her query, there is also an element of transparency that is built into the system. If the question asked by the farmer is not solved by the person attending on him at the call centre level (first level), then the question is escalated to the second level, consisting of agricultural officials where possible solution is given to the farmer. If the query is still not solved by the second level, a unique docket number is generated by the system and given to the farmer and the farmer is advised to call after some time with that docket number as a reference so that the best possible solution can be obtained from scientists and concerned department official. The citizen's charter system coupled with strong applications such as grievance monitoring system and call centre has resulted in increased level of responsiveness, accountability and transparency in government departments.

Lokvani Experiment in Uttar Pradesh

The Lokvani was initiated on 9 November 2004 in Sitapur, a district in Uttar Pradesh (UP), India, to empower citizens through the use of IT (information technology) and provide efficient administration at the district level (Griglani, 2006). The need for this system was felt due to the poor functioning of district administration with all its processes being manual processes. Due to bureaucratic and hierarchical model of functioning, even ordinary documents such as birth, death, domicile, caste and income certificates were difficult to obtain and were time-consuming processes. The citizens were allotted a fixed time of two hours to interact with the District Magistrate (administrative head of the district) for filing their complaints, which was often not sufficient, as a large number of complainants turned up. It was at this juncture the Lokvani project was conceived with the idea of inducting ICT (information and communication technology) to manage the delivery of services to all the citizens. As a part chain of 42-Lokvani kiosk centres were established throughout the district where people could access information regarding land records, arms licence application status, and provident fund accounts, medical facility and also file complaints to the District Magistrate by paying nominal fixed charges to kiosks. This system helped in streamlining the functioning of collectorate by reducing the response time, improving the efficiency and productivity of manpower in handling public grievances through Internet, and increasing their accountability to people (Annexure A-6.1: Lokvani Initiative).

The following services are offered through Lokvani centres:

- Online submission, monitoring and disposal of public grievances/complaints.
- Single window services.
- Birth certificates.
- Death certificates.
- Caste certificates.

- Income certificates.
- Domicile certificates.
- Tendering services.
- Status of arms licence applications.
- Information about local employment opportunities in the district.
- Online land records.
- Information about various government works, schemes, expenditures and beneficiaries.

The information related to various departments was made available to the kiosks through a website and the person manning would enter the complaint on behalf of the complainant. A copy of the complaint is given to the complainant along with an acknowledgement. These complaints are sent to the collectorate and marked to concerned officials. A timeframe is determined for resolving the complaints.

Online Grievance Redressal Tracking System in Andhra Pradesh

The GoAP initiated a system of grievance redressal by local government institutions using information technology (CGG, 2004). As local governments are closer to the people and are expected to be more responsive in addressing their needs and in providing services satisfactory to them, they have to constantly re-invent themselves to meet the ever rising demands of the society and citizens. As we are all aware, an important and integral aspect of municipal services is the redressal of grievances with respect to the delivery of civic services. The normal grievance process starts with a citizen registering a complaint in the municipal office verbally or through a written application to the concerned section, from where the complaint moves up through different channels to the Municipal Commissioner, who issues orders for necessary action by the official who is responsible. These orders move downwards through different channels for the action to be executed. This process of grievance handling is highly dependent upon the attitude of the machinery and grievance redressal takes place after a lot of persuasion by the citizen and the head/commissioner, as the official, is not accountable. The procedure is formal, long and time consuming. Therefore, alternative systems and means of improving the grievance redressal were tried out to help citizens as well as the administration to make administration more responsive and accountable. The Online Grievance Redressal Tracking System (OGRTS) used the IT systems and services to handle grievances in a much more effective manner. OGRTS was developed, tested and implemented successfully by the CGG, Hyderabad, as a pilot, in partnership with the Collectorate of Rangareddy District in AP under the mission-mode project of the GoI and the AP State Government.

The OGRTS was an attempt to automate the process of grievance handling and redressal, and to reduce the overheads for the government and citizens, thus reducing the frustration level among the citizens and to that extent increasing their satisfaction level. The basic objectives of the new grievance redressal mechanism that uses OGRTS were:

- To provide adequate ICT facilities for all users to ensure optimum usage of resources.
- To provide an excellent and effective user support/help desk.
- To provide access to information based on user privileges.
- To archive essential information for later retrieval and analysis.
- To connect the entire state in a single network.
- To provide an effective automated monitoring system.
- To integrate various communication channels: SMS (short message service), web, e-mail and post.
- To reduce delays due to physical transmission of the files.
- To use online systems based on open source technologies.
- To help citizens to fully utilise various services of the government and thereby improve their standard of living.

Later, OGRTS was successfully deployed in the municipalities of the district headquarters in all districts of AP, with the funding support of Andhra Pradesh Urban Services for the Poor (APUSP), the technical support of CGG and the facilitation/ownership of the urban local bodies of district headquarters. OGRTS was one of the first few initiatives in India which chartered a new direction in mobile government.

Steps Involved

- Registering grievance.
- Automatic forwarding to the functionary.
- Automatic escalation as per citizen's charter.
- Updation of action taken.
- Checking status.

Services Channels

A dedicated call centre managed the services and citizens could connect through a dedicated telephone number, email, internet and mobile.

Grievance handling under OGRTS is done through call centres, which act as the front offices, while the redressal is done by the back office which is the municipal office. Grievances are also registered online through the website of the portal and through the mobile phone. A docket number is created for each grievance registered. The OGRTS allows for classifying grievances based on the area, subject and functionary, and it forwards them to appropriate units/sections of the municipality for redressal. Once a complaint is forwarded, the functionary has to take action as per the time limits set out in the citizen's charter, failing which the complaint will escalate to the next higher level functionary. The functionary can update the status of the complaint at any level of the hierarchy, but once the complaint's action is updated as 'solved', no other functionary is allowed to change the status except the Regional Director. The higher level functionaries can view the action taken by the functionaries below their level. Any functionary can update the status of the complaint with a brief description of action taken either through SMS or through online application. The citizen can check the status of the complaint by calling the call centre with the docket number assigned to the grievance or by sending an SMS in the predefined format specifying the docket number.

Grievance Redressal System: A Case Study of a Tertiary Hospital in Andhra Pradesh

The case study described in this section is an initiative by the GoAP in "Establishing a Citizen Suggestion and Grievance Redressal System" (Geeta and Parigi, 2010) in a tertiary health service delivery facility (Gandhi Hospital) in Hyderabad. This initiative is a part of the health sector reforms programme of GoAP with financial assistance from Department for International Development (DFID), UK. The main objective of this pilot initiative was to provide information to the patients/attendants about the various services available at the hospital and create a channel/forum to register their grievances and assist in effective redressal.

Preparatory Work

Initial Sensitisation

There was an intensive preparatory work done prior to the launching of the pilot. Series of meetings were held with the Superintendent and hospital staff to develop a common understanding of the pilot and its benefits. Consultations were held with representatives of the nurses associations, junior doctors, key administrative staff, resident medical officers, patient attendants, and select NGOs to bring them on board regarding the study and initiation of this pilot. It was a very essential step in order to avoid misconception among the hospital staff that this pilot was meant to identify the problems in the hospital and bring to light the existing problems with service delivery. Wide range of consultations was also held across a broad spectrum of patients from both IP (inpatient) and OP (outpatient) wards to understand the needs of the patients and their grievances with service delivery.

As a part of the mechanism for evolving an appropriate design of the system and to provide internal support to the project, a Grievance Redressal Task Force (GRTF) was set up in July 2009, with Superintendent as the Chairman of the Task Force and Resident

Medical Officer as the convenor. The GRTF has been the major force in providing the necessary impetus for the implementation of the project.

In order to design an effective grievance redressal system for the hospital, it was essential to understand the problem areas in the hospital. It was essential to primarily understand the problems that the patients face in the hospital, especially the inpatients. An attempt was made to gather information on grievances that have been received by the hospital during the last 3-5 years. In the absence of any recorded data, it was difficult to undertake any meaningful analysis of the nature of grievances arising in Gandhi Hospital, therefore a quick snap survey was done to elicit opinion of the patients on the services provided by the hospital including treatment by the doctor, nursing care, and services from *ayahs* and ward boys, hygiene, food, medicines, diagnostic tests, facilities for the attendants and other related aspects.

Methodology

Considering the time and cost involved, it was decided to interview 300 patients: 150 from IPs and 150 from OPs. The sample of IPs was taken from the patients discharged after treatment every day. The sample of OPs was taken from the OP wards of different specialisations. Five investigators and one field coordinator were deployed to meet the sample patients/attendants and collect the information on structure questionnaires. Two separate questionnaires—one for IPs and another for OPs were prepared. As some of the specialisations in outpatients were weekly—once or twice—the field data collection was spread over 7 days. Regarding inpatients, the sample was taken from the discharged patients every day and the fieldwork was spread over 10 days (Annexure A-6.3).

Sample Profile

A total of 304 patients were actually interviewed: 150 IPs and 154 OPs. The number of patients interviewed in each specialisation is given in Table 6.1.

Table 6.1

Number of Patients Interviewed by Specialisation

Inpatients			*Outpatients*		
1	Medical	57	1	Urology	10
2	Gynaecology	31	2	Neuro Physician	12
3	Orthopaedics	18	3	Paediatrics and Paediatric Surgery	32
4	Surgical	15	4	Endocrinology	10
5	Paediatrics	1	5	Gastroenterology	8
6	Neuro Surgical	4	6	Cardiology	14
7	CT Surgery	11	7	Medicine	24
8	Cardiology	13	8	Orthopaedics	21
	Total	150	9	Gynaecology	23
				Total	15

Identification of Grievances Arising in the Hospital

Based on the survey conducted, a brief questionnaire was made to get responses from the patients on various aspects like quality of service delivery, the grievances that have been reported by patients for both IPs and OPs (For details see Annexure A-6.3).

Designing the Pilot

The grievance redressal system that was designed for Gandhi Hospital was a comprehensive one with a robust front end design which included information boards, display boards, help desks and trained personnel at the desk to provide requisite information. Appropriate procedures for grievance redressal were developed as a part of the design. Monitoring systems were also put in place to ensure smooth functioning of the pilot.

The project enhanced to a great extent accountability levels within the organisation. The GRTF and the senior management in the hospital were completely involved during the design phase of the pilot to ensure that a system which is more user-friendly can be put in place. The Resident Medical Officer who was the nodal officer involved himself on a daily basis to oversee the day-to-day functioning of the system and to ensure that the redressal of the grievance arising from the patients and their attendants was dealt in a satisfactory manner.

Figure 6.1

A Diagrammatic Representation of the Model of GR System

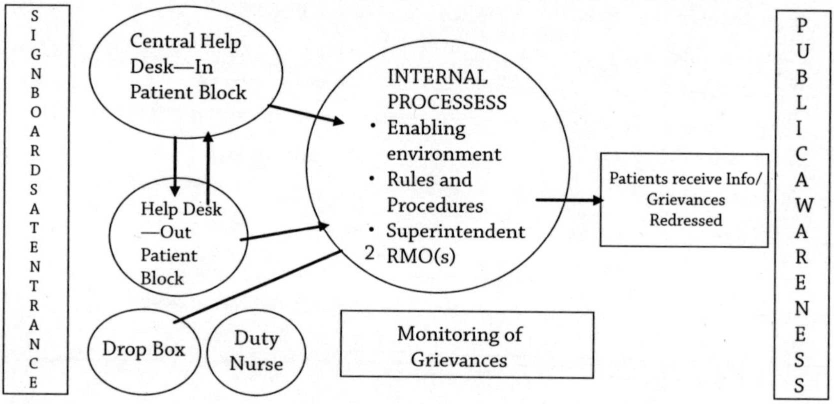

Front End

The front end includes:

- Help desk at IP and OP block.
- Help desk assistants to man the desks at IP and OP (6+1 Coordinator).
- Information on services available at the hospital.

Availability of Information

Information is the key for the functioning of the help desk. At the help desk, information was made available in English, Telugu and Urdu.

- Citizen's Charters (A Guide for Patients).
- Display of Service available at the Desk.
- Grievance forms/Feedback forms.
- Suggestion boxes.
- Banners.
- Floor-wise information and telephone numbers of doctors and other key personnel.

- Register for recording grievances.
- Leaflets on guidance to patients.

Annexures A-6.4a, A-6.4b and A-6.4c provide the information made available at the front desk.

Help Desk at Outpatient

A help desk was set up at the OP building. The desk was manned by two help desk assistants who worked from 8.30 am to 2.00 pm (during the working hours at the OP department).

Help Desk at Inpatient

A help desk was set up at the entrance of the IP building, which was managed by two help desk assistants on all days of the week, from 8.00 am to 5.00 pm, and one assistant each, from 5.00 pm to 1.00 am, and another from 1.00 am to 8.00 am. A supervisor was also appointed to ensure smooth functioning of the help desk. The help desk was fully equipped with a computer with Internet facility and a printer and a separate telephone line. Apart from providing information to the patients on various services available at the hospital, the help desk personnel also provide information to the patients as well as assist them in locating the wards, and directing the patients to their respective destinations. The help desk assistants also provided special assistance to elderly and physically handicapped patients. The help desk also assisted the illiterate patients to put their grievances in a written form. The help desk supervisor and staff met the concerned authorities at regular intervals and brought to their notice the various problems faced by the patients and kept in touch with the Resident Medical Officer and the Superintendent of the hospital on a daily basis.

Grievance Redressal Procedure

In order to provide effective grievance redressal system, the basic systems and procedures were formalised and put in place. The Superintendent of Gandhi Hospital released circulars to all the concerned persons at various levels on their duties and responsibilities. Thus, a consolidated grievance redressal procedure was evolved by identifying specific grievance areas and remedial steps to be taken by the concerned staff within specified time frames for acting on the grievances relieved (See Annexure A-6.5 for consolidated procedures developed for running the pilot). Extensive consultation was carried out before finalising the grievance redressal procedure for the hospital. Sensitisation programmes were also organised for the service delivery staff at various levels on the responsibilities and timelines for grievance redressal indicated in the procedures outlined as a part of the system.

Citizen's Charters

One of the key activities that was taken up during the project period was development of a Patient Guide (Citizen's Guide/Charter) which provides at one point all the information regarding the services available at Gandhi Hospital. The guide was made available at the help desk in local language. The guide provides information regarding floor-wise details of the building, room numbers, details of doctor including their telephone numbers, timing of doctors and others. The guide also provides information about lab timings and persons responsible for the lab (Annexure A-6.6).

Formats and Registers

Patient grievance redress forms were developed and kept at the help desk. The forms were made in local language. In order to streamline record keeping, various formats were also developed for registering the grievance by the help desk assistants.

The help desk at OP desk was made operational from 23 January 2010 and the IP desk was started on 3 February 2010. After a period of three months, a review was done to examine by an independent group consisting of NGOs, representatives from the funding agency, to assess the effectiveness of the system that was put in place. Besides receiving oral complaints on cleanliness in wards, toilets, the following written complaints were received during the 3 months period of the operationalisation of the help desk:

- Around 150-160 enquiries has been attended daily at the help desks.

- Around 38 complaints had been received from OP and IP during the period.
- The main categories of grievances are related to:
  - Non-availability of medicines and X-ray films (11).
  - Problems at registration counter: slips not stamped at OP registration (2).
  - Lab not being open during working hours (7).
  - Doctor not available and not treating on time (5).
  - Lack of wheel chairs and stretchers (2).
  - Bad infrastructure facilities at waiting hall in OP (broken foot holds for benches, no drinking water, no fans, lights) (7).
  - Lack of cleanliness (bathrooms and toilets not clean).
  - Rude behaviour of staff (1).
  - Corruption (3).

Lessons Leant

Although the hospital evolved a comprehensive grievance redressal procedure with timeframes and authorities responsible for redressal, there are a number of gaps in the implementation of the system.

Disposal Process (Issues and Challenges)

As per the design, as and when the complaints are received at the help desk/suggestion box, the complaints are handed over on a daily basis to the concerned Resident Medical Officer who is the convenor of the Task Force. The time frame designed for grievance redressal was felt to be much slower, which needed to be sped up for enhancing efficiency of disposal of complaints.

Internal Procedures

It was felt that there is a need for the hospital authorities to adhere strictly to the timelines and internal procedures developed by themselves for effectiveness of the pilot. If these timelines and procedures are adhered to strictly, and regular review on the time taken for disposal of complaints is done by higher authorities, only then will the grievance redressal system work effectively.

Systemic Changes Required

The analysis of the grievances shows that a large number of grievances are related to lack of infrastructure, HR issues, attitudinal problems of the staff, lack of strict internal monitoring, and corruption. It becomes critical for the superintendent of the hospital to personally take up these issues with the Department of Medical Education and the state government and bring these to the notice of the higher authorities for necessary intervention.

Need for Strengthening Accountability

The internal procedure that had been developed by the Hospital Authorities with specific responsibilities given to staff at various levels need to be strictly implemented as it has a capacity tool fix responsibilities and make individual staff accountable for their lapses in providing services to the patients.

Monitoring Mechanisms

The review mechanisms put in place for the pilot include regular reviews by the Task Force, Superintendent, HDS and the Government.

- The help desk will hand over the complaints received to the concerned nodal officer and update the Superintendent at the end of each day.
- Weekly review on every Tuesday at 2:00 pm with Superintendent, Nodal officer and HD coordinator on the progress made.
- A monthly report on the nature of grievances will be generated by the help desk. The Task Force will convene once in a month to review the information.
- The Hospital Development Society will be presented with the reports on monthly basis and will be updated about the progress.
- Regular monitoring and review of the system is required. Quarterly report to be prepared by the GRTF and to be sent to Secretary, HDS and others.

Institutional Machinery for Oversight

Audit Mechanisms

Third party audit mechanism can be a very crucial element in this whole project. Accountability levels can be improved and sustained to a great extent if stakeholders are involved and are given a mandate to review the services being offered at the hospital. Although administrative audit are to be done regularly by the hospital authorities, to assess the nature of grievances received by the hospital and mechanism to deal with them, the real impact will be visible when there is a third party audit mechanism in place.

Ombudsman

Setting up an ombudsman could be a good option for effective grievance redressal of patients just like in case of insurance, banking, income tax and others. The Government of Kerala has an ombudsman for dealing with citizen grievances with regard to the services rendered by local bodies in the state.

Hospital Development Society and Grievance Redressal Task Force

The Hospital Development Society is an oversight body which has members from people's representatives (local body members), prominent citizens and others. This institution has a mandate to ensure that the hospitals are delivering satisfactory services to the citizens. Therefore, it is important to rope them into regular monitoring and review of the functioning of the hospital as well as grievance redressal issues which can be taken up on a regular basis. It will also be very useful if a Class IV employee representative can be made a part of the GRTF team so that they are made aware of the grievances and deficiencies in their staff's performance.

Effective Information Dissemination

It was observed that there were some gaps in communication which were being sent out to the patient through a post card informing about the redressal of their grievance. In order to disseminate information more effectively, an in-house journal type of an initiative needs to be taken up by the hospital as a tool for communication.

Various initiatives relating to patient improvement services can be documented and disseminated to the larger public. It will also be relevant if annual report on the grievances received and redressed is to be published and brought out by the hospital for wider dissemination. This report can also be placed on the website.

Behavioural Accountability

Serious nature of grievances received against the staff (serious misconduct) to be made a part of their personal file and recorded in their performance review. This will ensure greater accountability. There is a need to provide incentives to departments/units which provide satisfactory services and meet the expectations of the patients.

Performance Accountability

There are allotted responsibilities for functionaries at various levels in the hospital for the sake for proper service delivery, upkeep and maintenance of each floor such as sanitation, water supply, electricity, etc., so as to ensure effective maintenance of utilities. However, it is expected that they effectively undertake their responsibilities, failure to do so must be viewed seriously by the higher authorities, thus, enhancing their performance accountability to the fullest extent.

Motivation and Behavioural Change

For effective communication and service delivery to the patients, there is a need for continuous sensitisation of the staff, right from Class IV to the top management on communication, behavioural and attitudinal skills/changes. There is also a need for a full-time coordinator of patient services to monitor the work of help desk functions, processing of grievances, providing feedback to the hospital authorities, communication of final decision on the resolving of grievances to patients and all other related activities.

Manpower Issues

There are a number of HR issues in the organisation that need to be fixed for effective implementation of the grievance redressal system. Some of the specific HR issues are as follows:

- There are a number of posts of the Medico Social workers which are currently vacant in Gandhi Hospital, which are to be filled up. These persons will be employed for counselling the patients and attendants on their visits to the wards, and also function as coordinators between the patients, the doctors and nurses.
- A separate full-time coordinator to be appointed to be in-charge of patient relation, monitor the work of help desk functions, processing of grievances, providing feedback to the hospital authorities, communication of final decision on the resolving of grievances to patients and all other related activities.
- The coordinator will also be responsible for the conduct of the third party led audit, scaling up of operations of the help desk and also in other tertiary hospitals in the state.
- Class IV staff play a key role in providing services to patients and a number of gaps are found in this area. It is suggested that discussions are held with Class IV union leaders on the need to take care of patients needs promptly so that patients have no grouse to complaint against them.

In Conclusion

The pilot initiative taken up by the government of Andhra Pradesh has thrown up a number of issues related to systemic challenges in health service delivery. This experiment has brought to light some very interesting observations which indicate that streamlining service delivery to the poor is an activity that requires commitment, transparency, accountability and compassion on the part of the service provider. More than anything else, it is the intent of the government to serve the public and this pilot has demonstrated that there is immense scope of improving health service delivery to the poor.

References

Centre for Good Governance (2004). *Collected Working Papers.* Vol 1 & 2. Dr MCR HRD IAP, Hyderabad.

Geeta, P. (2001). *A Brief on the Training on Citizen's Charters and Social Accountability for the Participants of CESSD, Project.* Government of Pakistan, funded by World Bank, New Delhi.

Griglani, C. (2006). *A Report on Grievance Redressal System in Government.* Submitted to DFID. Hyderabad: Institute of Public Enterprise.

Geeta, P. and Parigi V.K. (2010). *A Report on Establishing a Grievance Redressal System in Tertiary Hospital in Andhra Pradesh.* Project funded by DFID UK.

Annexure A-6.1

Lokvani Initiative

Lokvani is an e-governance initiative by the combined efforts of District Administration and National Informatics Centre in Sitapur (UP, India). The initiative is not only giving a practical shape to the Right to Information Act, but is also creating job opportunities for the educated but unemployed youth of Sitapur. Lokvani is a unique public private partnership program, which gives citizens an opportunity to interact with the government without coming to any government office.

Lokvani was conceptualised by District Magistrate, Sitapur in September 2004. He commissioned a study of similar initiatives in the districts of Jhalawad (Rajasthan) and Dhar (Madhya Pradesh). The study revealed the strengths and weaknesses of these efforts; Lokvani was accordingly designed to improve upon them.

A society by the name Lokvani was constituted to implement the project autonomously and to reduce the bureaucratic hassles. The National Informatics Centre (NIC) provided the necessary technical know-how for the project. It was decided that instead of opening new kiosks, existing cyber cafes/computer training institutes should be granted licenses to become Lokvani Centres. This decision was taken to ensure the financial viability and the long-term sustainability of the kiosks.

The information related to various departments was made available to the kiosks through a website hosted on NIC Delhi web server. The kiosks were given login/passwords to log on to Lokvani website. The Rate List for the services was finalized and care was taken to ensure that the kiosks follow the prescribed pricing.

By December 2004, 13 Lokvani Centres were set up. As on June 2008, the number has gone up to 115. Instead of coming all the way to the District Office the citizens can now avail several government services at the *tehsil*, block and town level itself. Lokvani can be accessed on the Internet at *www.sitapur.nic.in/lokvani* (User Name: guest, Password: guest). Services/information like Land Records, Tender Forms, Employment Information, FPS allotments, Arms licence application status, GPF accounts of basic education teachers are available online now. To ensure transparency, details of developmental works, ration allotment to fair price shop dealers, money sent to *Gram Sabhas* etc. are made available to people. The most popular service till date has been Online Public Grievance Redressal, which has received more than 1,17,179 complaints by 15 June 2008 of which 1,13,793

(97%) has been disposed off. The Lokvani system not only gives citizens an avenue to track the progress on their grievance, but also provides the DM an effective tool to monitor the performance of various departments. Lokvani also provides details of various government schemes, government prescribed forms, details of developmental work in the district, lists of old age pensioners, lists of scholarship beneficiaries, Funds allotted in various government schemes, allotment of food grains to *kotedars*, allotments of funds to *gram panchayats* etc.

The land records have been computerised and available on line at Lokvani website. Also services like Online Registration of Death/Births, Certificates for SC/STs, Domicile etc being offered through Single Window service. 59 other districts of UP have already started implementing Lokvani based citizen services. Going forward, the kiosks are being opened at the Nyay Panchayat level to increase the reach of the service. Government of U.P. has issued a G.O. on 16-06-2005 to replicate Lokvani in the entire state.

The Challenges for the Lokvani are however not few. The system has to evolve in a way so as to reduce the dependence on the DM's direct interest in the project. This is possible if DM's progress is monitored and compared at the state level. State level monitoring tool has been developed for this purpose, where status of all districts of UP can be monitored. The state level status of Lokvani can be seen at *http://sitapur.nic.in/lokvani/lokvaniupreport.asp*. The financial viability of the kiosks at the village level is a hurdle, which can be overcome by creative ways to distribute services and commercial products.

The longest journeys in life begin with the first step; Lokvani has laid a firm foundation for the e-governance in Uttar Pradesh. It is hoped that it would be a torchbearer for other such G2C efforts across the country.

Contact Persons

1. Amod Kumar, Sp. Secy IT & Electronics, GoUP, Lucknow. Ph: (0522) 2237006
2. A.P. Singh, Technical Director-NIC, Sitapur. Ph: 242250 (O)
3. Devendra Kr. Pandey, Sub Divisional Magistrate, Jaunpur. Ph: 9415053416 (M)

Annexure A-6.2

Grievances on Services at Gandhi Hospital—Inpatient

S. No.	*Nature of Grievances*
A.	**Doctors**
1.	Doctors have no patience to listen to us and answer our queries/doubts
2.	Doctors did not attend to our satisfaction or attended lately
3.	Doctors have not explained in detail about the disease and treatment
4.	Doctors are not polite and courteous
B.	**Nurses**
1.	Nurses are not polite and courteous
2.	Nurses do not attend patients promptly
C.	**Ayahs and Ward Boys**
1.	*Ayahs* and ward boys are not polite and courteous
2.	*Ayahs* and ward boys demand money for providing services otherwise they provide services reluctantly
D.	**Services related to Cot, Bed and Bed sheet**
1.	Cots are broken or unhygienic
2.	Bed and bed sheets are torn, dirty and unhygienic
3.	Bed sheets are never changed or changed occasionally
E.	**Ward, Rooms and Toilets**
1.	Wards/rooms are very dirty and bad
2.	Toilets are very dirty and bad
3.	Number of toilets are not adequate
F.	**Diagnostic Test and Medicines**
1.	Diagnostic Tests are not done at the hospital and have to be done outside by patients
2.	Most medicines and injections are not available in the hospital and have to be procured from outside
G.	**Drinking Water and Food Supplied for Patient**
1.	Food supplied is of very poor quality
2.	Pure drinking water is not available only *nala* (from the toilet) water
3.	Bring water from home
H.	**Amenities for Attendants**
1.	Amenities for attendants are very poor
2.	Quality of canteen food is poor

contd...

...contd...

I.	**Security in the Hospital and Behaviour of Security Guards**
1.	Security in the hospital is very poor
2.	Security guards at the entrance demand money
J.	**Admission and Registration**
1.	Patients have to wait for long to complete the admission formalities
2.	More than one visit to be made for completing admission formalities
3.	Problem in locating the proper counter for registration
4.	Directional boards are not seen
5.	No proper guidance available
6.	Counter staff are rude
7.	Counter staff are polite and courteous
K.	**Parking Facility**
1.	Adequate parking facility is not available
2.	No comments on parking facility as we do not require
3.	Ward boys/*Ayahs* demand money for providing wheelchair/stretcher
L.	**Security Guards**
1.	Security staff at entrance are rude and blunt
2.	Security staff at entrance demand money

Grievances on Services at Gandhi Hospital—Outpatient

S. No.	*Details*
A.	**Doctors**
1.	Doctors do not explain in detail about the disease and treatment
2.	Doctors have no patience to listen to us and answer our queries/doubts
3.	Doctors are not polite and courteous
B.	**Nurses**
1.	Nurses are not polite and courteous
2.	Nurses demand money for providing service every time a service is requested
C.	**Diagnostic Test**
1.	Diagnostic tests are not done at the hospital and have to be done outside by patients
2.	Most medicines and injections are available and have to be procured from outside

contd...

...contd...

D.	**Neatness and cleanliness of OP ward and toilets**
1.	OP hall dirty and bad
2.	Toilets are dirty and bad
3.	Toilets are not adequate in the OP hall
E.	**Provision of drinking water and quality of canteen food**
1.	No drinking water facility at OP hall
2.	Quality of canteen food is poor
F.	**Registration process**
1.	Takes a lot of time to complete the registration formalities
2.	Need to visit more than one window for completing the registration
3.	Long queue at every window
4.	Difficulty in locating the proper counter
5.	Directional boards are not seen
6.	No proper guidance at the registration counter
7.	Counter staff are rude
G.	**Provision of Wheelchairs**
1.	Ward boys demand money for providing wheelchair/stretcher
2.	Adequate wheelchairs are not provided
3.	Adequate seats are not provided for patients/attendants
H.	**Consultation with Doctors**
1.	Doctors are not available on time
2.	Long waiting hours to meet the doctor
3.	No proper queue system at doctor's consultation room
4.	Nurses allow some to meet doctor out of turn
I.	**Parking Facility**
1.	Adequate parking facility is available
2.	No comments on parking facility as we do not require
J.	**Security Guards**
1.	Security staff at entrance are polite and courteous
2.	Security staff at entrance are rude and blunt
3.	Security staff at entrance demand money

Annexure A-6.3

Andhra Pradesh Health Sector Reform Programme (APHSRP): Identification of Nature of Grievances in Gandhi Hospital

Family Health International (December 2009)

1. Identification of Nature of Grievances in Gandhi Hospital

1.1 Backdrop

Under the APHSRP, a pilot on the grievance redressal system has been initiated in Gandhi Hospital. As a part of the pilot project, an attempt has been made to study the nature of grievances arising with regard to service delivery to the patients. A brief survey was conducted to understand the nature of grievances in Gandhi Hospital. The findings are presented as below.

1.2 Nature of Grievances

In the absence of any data, it was difficult to undertake any analysis of the nature of grievances arising in Gandhi Hospital. A quick snap survey was planned and executed to elicit opinion of the patients on the services provided by the hospital including treatment by the doctor, nursing care, and services from *ayahs* and ward boys, hygiene, food, medicines, diagnostic tests, facilities for the attendants and other related aspects.

1.3 Methodology

Considering the time and cost involved, it was decided to interview 300 patients—150 inpatients and 150 outpatients. The sample of inpatients was taken from the patients discharged after treatment every day. The sample of outpatients was taken from the outpatient wards of different specialisations. Five investigators and one field coordinator were deployed to meet the sample patients/ attendants and collect the information on structure questionnaires. Two separate questionnaires—one for inpatients and another for outpatients was prepared. As some of the specialisations in outpatients are weekly (once or twice), the field data collection was spread over 7 days. Regarding inpatients, the sample was taken from the discharged patients every day and the fieldwork was spread over 10 days.

1.4 Sample Profile

A total of 304 patients were actually interviewed—150 inpatients and 154 outpatients. The number of patients interviewed in each specialisation is given in Table 1.

Table 1

Number of Patients Interviewed by Specialisation

	Inpatients			*Outpatients*	
1	Medical	57	1	Urology	10
2	Gynecology	31	2	Neuro Physician	12
3	Orthopedics	18	3	Pediatrics & Pediatric Surgery	32
4	Surgical	15	4	Endocrinology	10
5	Pediatrics	1	5	Gastroenterology	8
6	Neuro Surgical	4	6	Cardiology	14
7	CT Surgery	11	7	Medicine	24
8	Cardiology	13	8	Orthopedics	21
	Total	150	9	Gynecology	23
				Total	154

2. Summary of Grievances

2.1 Grievances

The grievances as reported by patients are listed separately for inpatients and outpatients.

2.2 Inpatient

S. No	*Nature of Grievances*
1	**Doctors**
1	Doctors have no patience to listen to us and answer our queries/doubts
2	Doctors did not attend to our satisfaction or attended late
3	Doctors have not explained in detail about the disease and treatment
4	Doctors are not polite and courteous
2	**Nurses**
1	Nurses are not polite and courteous
2	Nurses do not attend patients promptly

contd...

3	**Ayahs and Ward boys**
1	*Ayahs* and Ward boys are not polite and courteous
2	*Ayahs* and Ward boys demand money for providing services otherwise they provide services reluctantly
4	**Services related to Cot, Bed and Bedsheet**
1	Cots are broke and unhygienic
2	Bed and bedsheets are torn, dirty and unhygienic
3	Bedsheets are never changed or changed occasionally
5	**Ward, Rooms and Toilets**
1	Wards/rooms are very dirty and bad
2	Toilets are very dirty and bad
3	Number of toilets are not adequate
6	**Diagnostic Test and Medicines**
1	Diagnostic tests are not done at the hospital and have to be done outside by patients
2	Most medicines and injections are not available in the hospital and have to be procured from outside
7	**Drinking Water and Food Supplied for Patient**
1	Food supplied is of very poor quality
2	Pure drinking water is not available only *Nala* (from the toilet) water
3	Bring water from home
8	**Amenities for Attendants**
1	Amenities for attendants are very poor
2	Quality of canteen food is poor
9	**Security in the hospital and behaviour of Security Guards**
1	Security in the hospital is very poor
2	Security guard at the entrance demand money
10	**Admission and Registration**
1	Patients have to wait for long to complete the admission formalities
2	More than one visit to be made for completing admission formalities
3	Problem in locating the proper counter for registration
4	Directional boards are not seen

S. No	Nature of Grievances
5	No proper guidance available
6	Counter staff are rude
7	Counter staff are polite and courteous
11	**Parking Facility**
1	Adequate parking facility is not available
2	No comments on parking facility as we do not require
3	Ward boys/*Ayahs* demand money for providing wheel chair/stretcher
12	**Security Guards**
1	Security staff at entrance are rude and blunt
2	Security staff at entrance demand money

2.3 Grievances on services at Gandhi Hospital: Outpatient

S. No	Details
1	**Doctors**
1	Doctors do not explain in detail about the disease and treatment
2	Doctors have no patience to listen to us and answer our queries/doubts
3	Doctors are not polite and courteous
2	**Nurses**
1	Nurses are not polite and courteous
2	Nurses demand money for providing service every time a service is requested
3	**Diagnostic Test**
1	Diagnostic tests are not done at the hospital and have to be done outside by patients
2	Most medicines and injections are not available and have to be procured from outside
4	**Neatness and cleanliness of OP ward and toilets**
1	OP hall dirty and bad
2	Toilets are dirty and bad
3	Toilets are not adequate in the OP hall
5	**Provision of drinking water and quality of canteen food**
1	No drinking water facility at OP hall
2	Quality of canteen food is poor
6	**Registration process**
1	Takes a lot of time to complete the registration formalities
2	Need to visit more than one window for completing the registration

contd...

...contd...

3	Long queue at every window
4	Difficulty in locating the proper counter
5	Directional boards are not seen
6	No proper guidance at the registration counter
7	Counter staff are rude
7	**Provision of Wheelchairs**
1	Ward boys demand money for providing wheelchair/stretcher
2	Adequate wheel chairs are not provided
3	Adequate seats are not provided for patients/attendants
8	**Consultation with Doctors**
1	Doctors are not available on time
2	Long waiting hours to meet the doctor
3	No proper queue system at doctor's consultation room
4	Nurses allow some to meet doctor out of turn
9	**Parking Facility**
1	Adequate parking facility is available
2	No comments on parking facility as we do not require
10	**Security Guards**
1	Security staff at entrance are polite and courteous
2	Security staff at entrance are rude and blunt
3	Security staff at entrance demand money

3. Grievances in Inpatients

The major grievances that have been identified from inpatients are presented below.

3.1 Grievances on Doctors: Inpatients

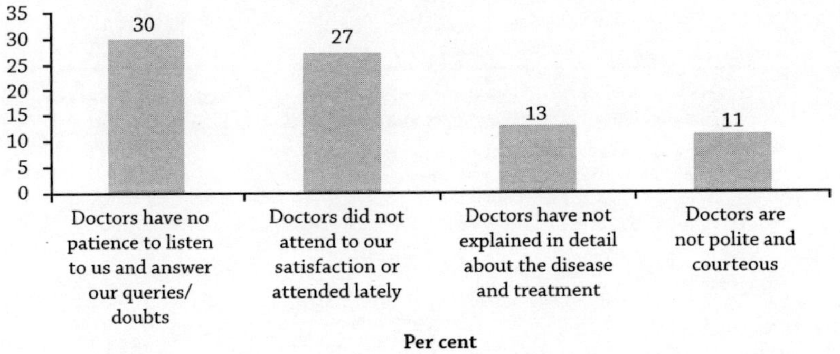

3.2 Grievances on Nurses: Inpatients

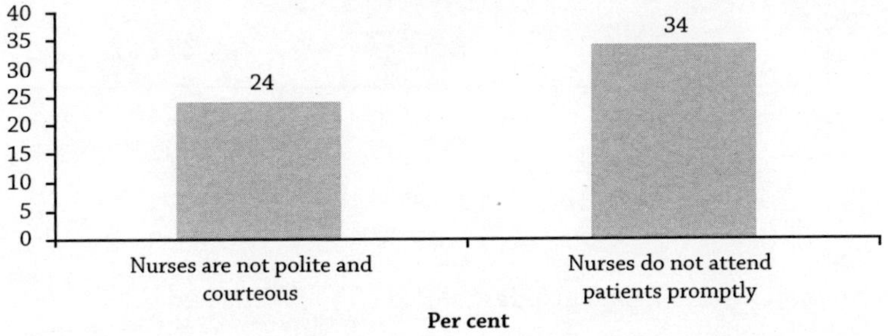

3.3 Grievances on Ayahs/Ward Boys: Inpatients

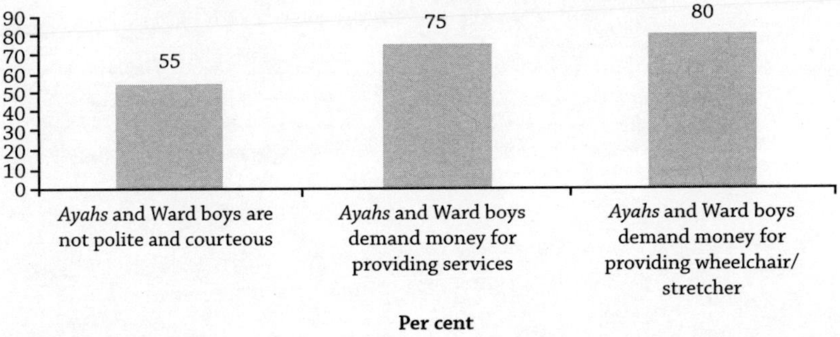

3.4 Complaints on Cot, Bed and Bed Sheets: Inpatients

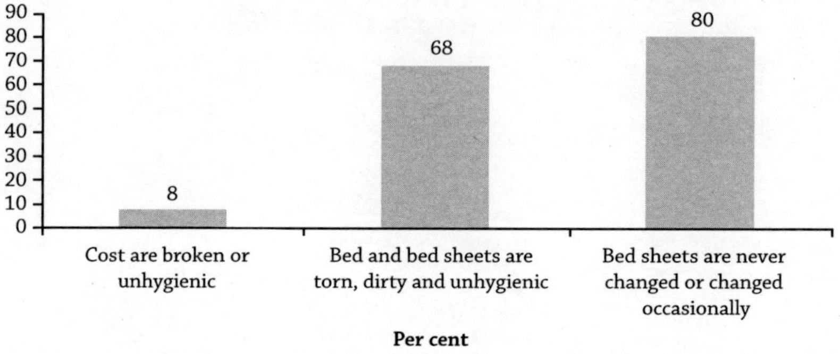

3.5 Cleanliness of Wards, Rooms and Toilets

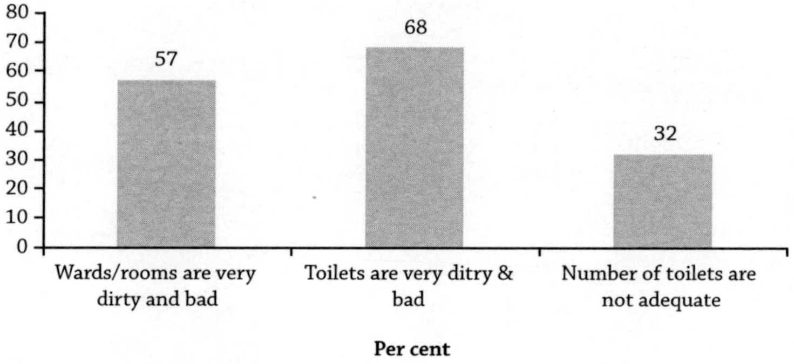

3.6 Diagnostic Test and Supply of Medicines

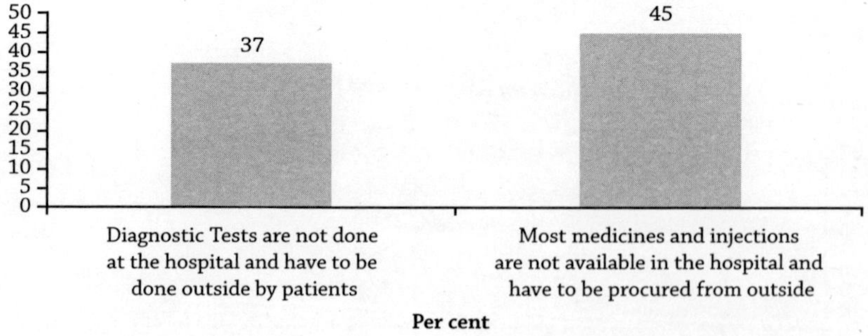

3.7 Drinking Water and Food Supplied for Patients

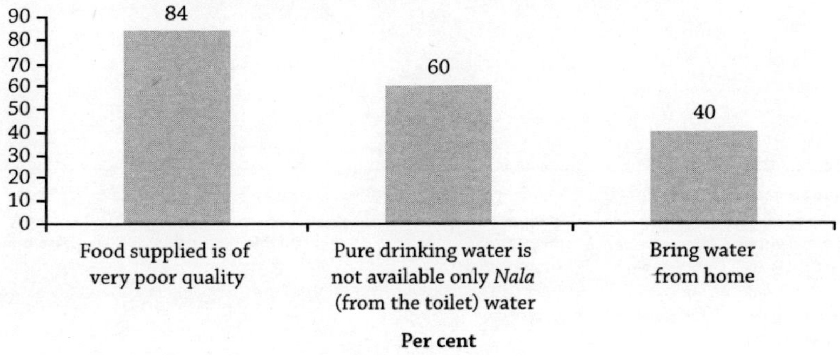

3.8 Amenities for Attendants

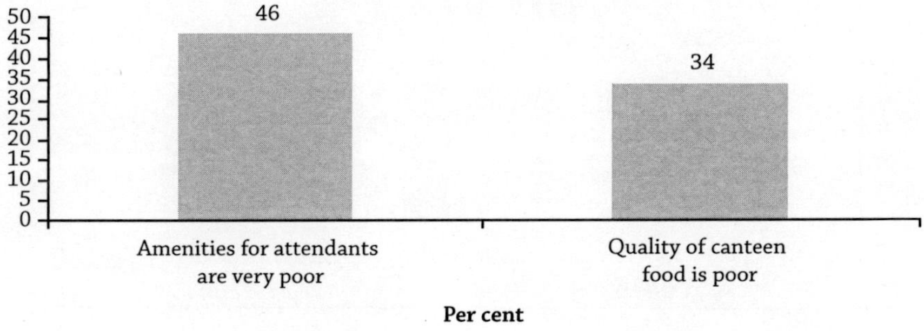

3.9 Grievances on Security Guards

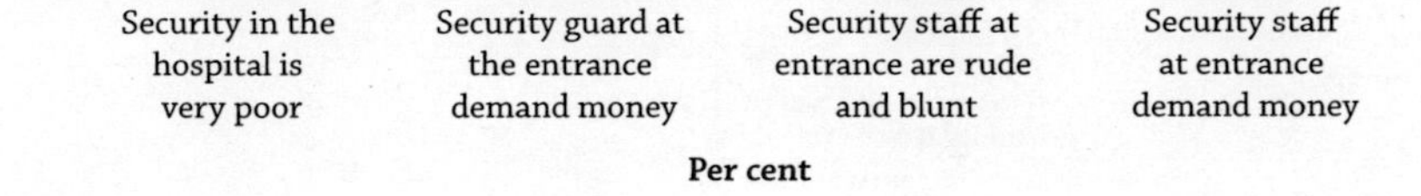

3.10 Grievances on Admission and Registration Process

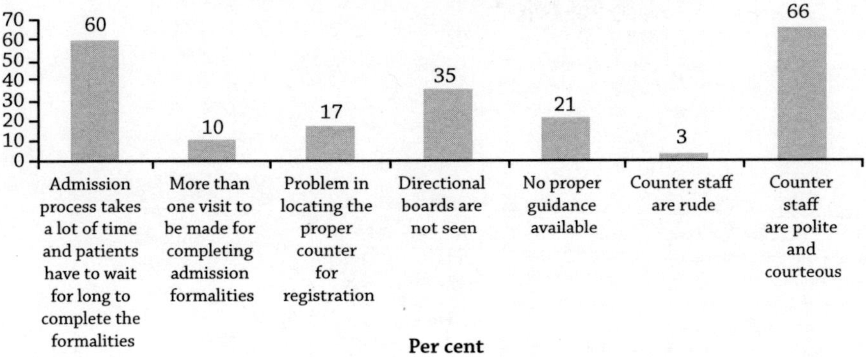

3.11 Parking Facility

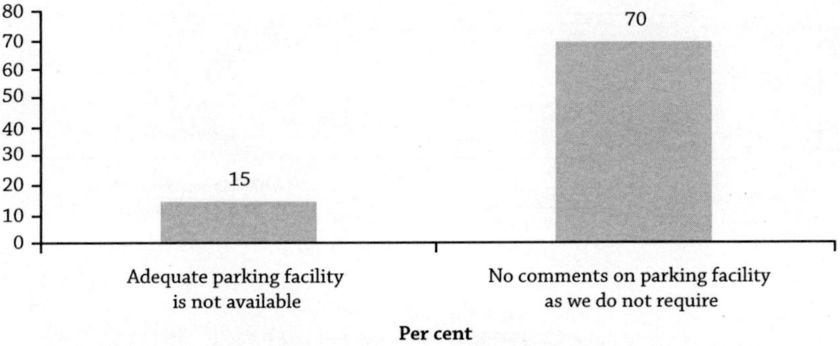

3.12 Reasons for Choosing Gandhi Hospital

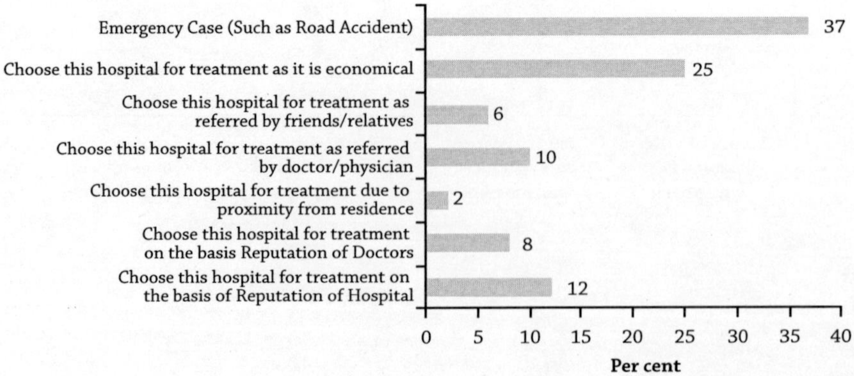

3.13 Overall Rating of Hospital

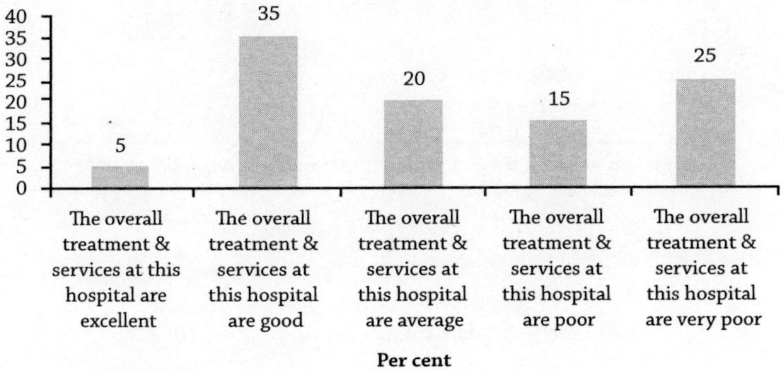

4. Grievances of Outpatients

The major grievances that have been identified from the outpatients are presented below.

4.1 Grievances on Doctors: Outpatient

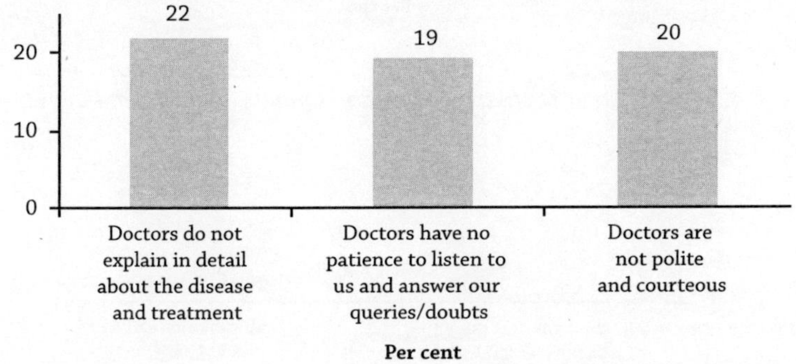

4.2 Grievances on Nurses: Outpatients

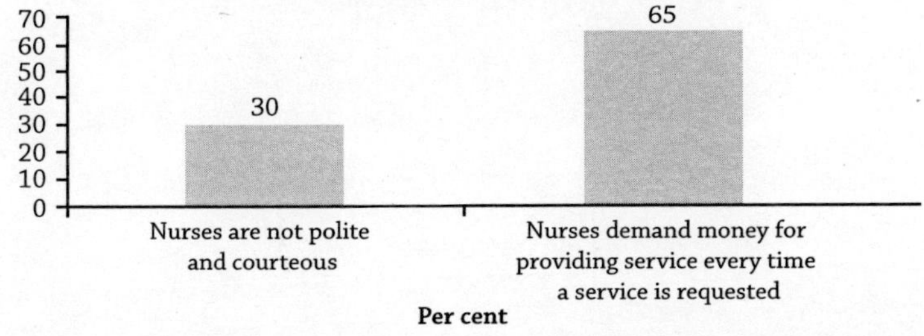

4.3 Diagnostic Test and Supply of Medicines

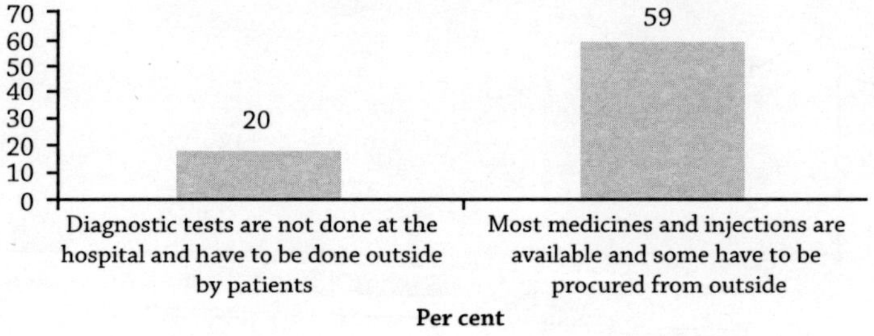

4.4 Neatness and Cleanliness of OP and Toilets

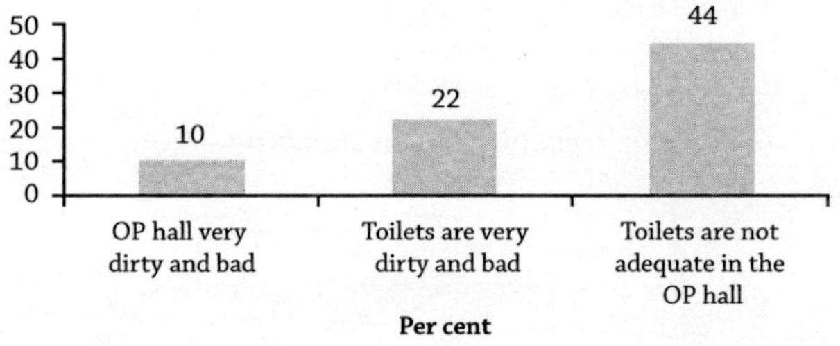

4.5 Provision of Drinking Water and Quality of Canteen Food

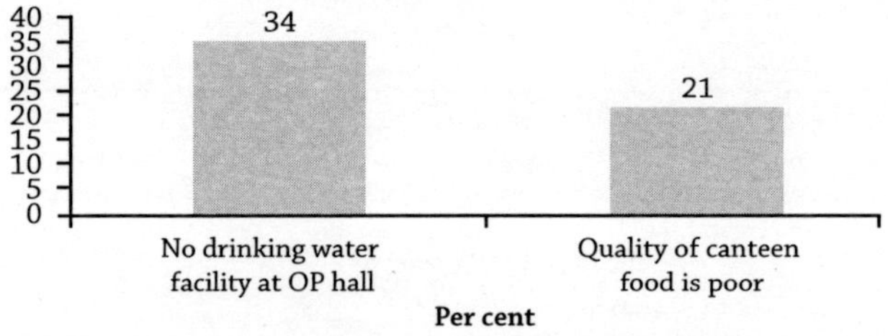

4.6 Registration Process

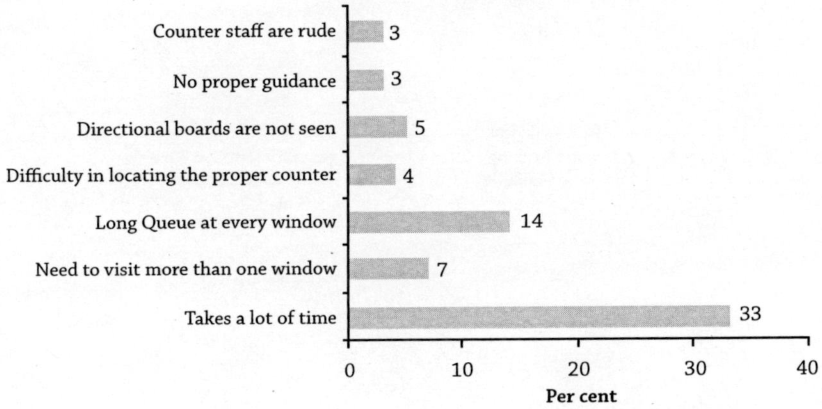

4.7 Provision of Seating and Wheelchairs

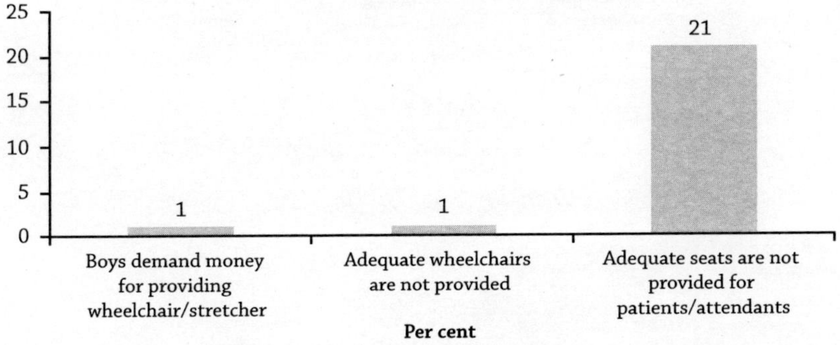

4.8 Consultation of Doctor

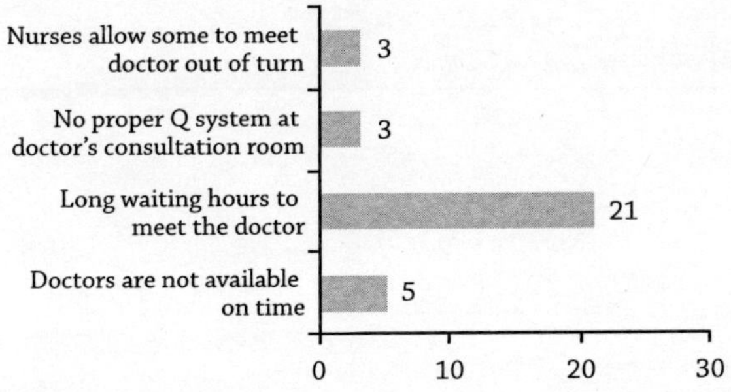

4.9 Parking Facility

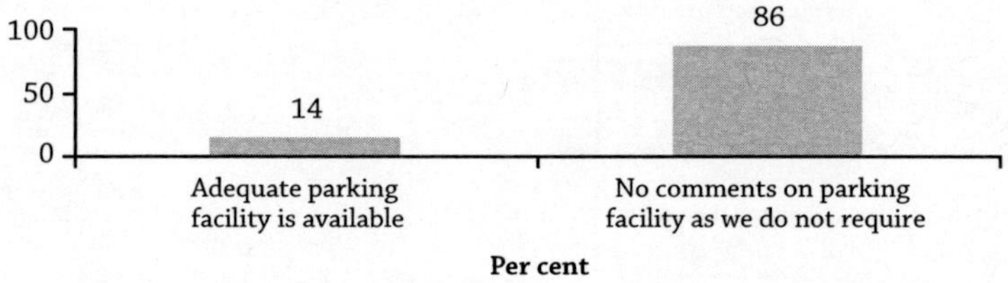

4.10 Security Guards

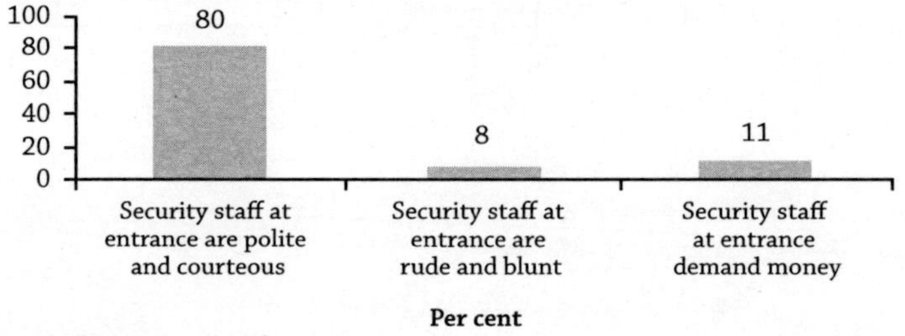

4.11 Reasons for Choosing Gandhi Hospital

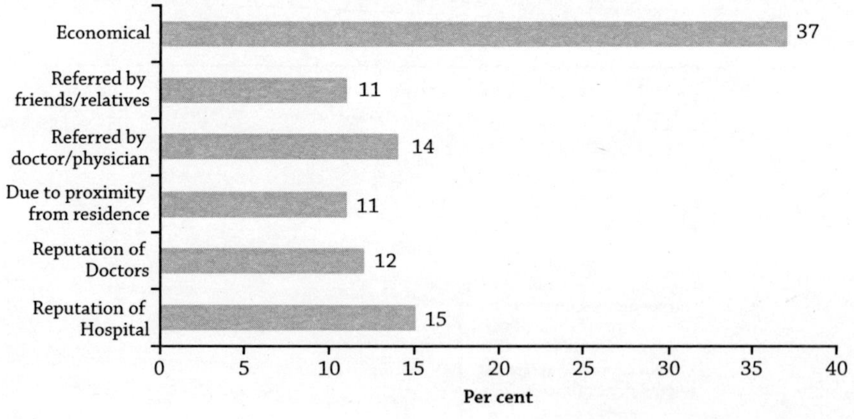

4.12 Overall Rating of Treatment and Services at Hospital

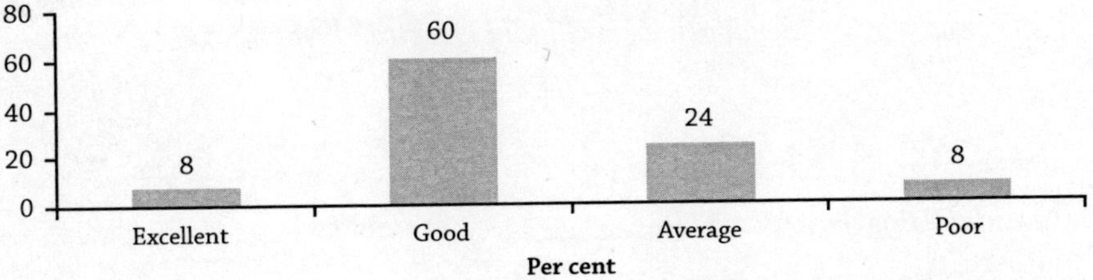

Annexure 6.4a

Patient Feedback form Gandhi Hospital, Hyderabad

S. No Date:

Place:

Outpatient/Inpatient Ward No.____________Speciality______________

1. Patient Registration Number
2. Name
3. Address
4. Phone No_____________Cell No.____________email____________
5. Please write your comments below on any aspect of service received by you during your stay in the Hospital (Quality of Service, Care, Courtesy of Staff, Cleanliness or any other area.

Please mention below the problems faced by you:

a) Getting admitted to the hospital? Yes/No

If yes, give details

b) In receiving treatment from the doctors/nurses? Yes/No

If yes, give details

c) In getting supply of medicines? Yes/No

If yes, give details

d) In getting tests done? Yes/No

If yes, give details

e) If you, faced any other problems please, write below.

6. Over all, were you satisfied with the services of the Hospital?

   Please Tick, (Yes / No)

   If yes, please rate the service (Please Tick your Answer)

   Very Good Good Average Poor

7. What are the services which require improvement? Please mention below

Name and signature of patient/attendant

We thank you for your response.

Annexure 6.4b

Grievance Redressal Register Format

S. No.	Form No.	Patient Registration No.	Name of the Patient	Address	Ward/ IP	Grievance Regarding	Forwarded To	Forwarded Date	Action taken	Remarks	Signature

Format for Grievances Received from Suggestion Boxes (7 boxes)

S. No.	Name of the Patient	Grievance Regarding	Forwarded To	Forwarded Date	Action taken	Remarks	Signature
1							
2							
3							
4							
5							
6							
7							

Summary Report

S. No.	Source for Receiving Grievances (suggestion boxes/feedback form)	Period from ----to ---- (7 days)	Name of the Complainant	Total Complaints Received	Total Grievances Redressed / Attended	Number of Grievances Pending	Remarks

Annexure 6.4c

Patient Grievance Form Gandhi Hospital, Hyderabad

Date:

Place:

1. Patient Registration Number
2. Name
3. Address
4. Phone No ------------------ Cell -------------------email-----------------------
5. Please give your ward details and date of Admission.

   ----

6. Please give below the details of your complaint/grievance.

Name and signature of the patient

Staff use only

Date Received:

Forwarded To:

Action Taken:

Further Action Required:

Signature of the staff

Acknowledgement to patient's complaint/grievance

S.No.

Date

Name of the Patient

Registration Number

Name and designation of Help Desk Staff/Hospital Staff

Annexure 6.5

Gandhi Hospital Hyderabad

Patients have the option to convey their grievances orally or in writing to the following authorities at Gandhi Hospital:

1. Head Nurse (in case the grievance arises from an Inpatient/Attendant)
2. Help Desk
3. Drop Box (the grievances form can be dropped in a Drop Box).

The grievances will be gathered from all the three sources mentioned above. In order to redress the grievances of the patients/attendants, a detailed procedure has been laid down by the hospital administration in a consultative manner.

The procedure has been presented below in the matrix:

Inpatient Grievance Redressal Procedure

S. No.	*Nature of Grievance*	*First Level Contact*	*Second Level Contact*	*Third Level Contact*	*Time Line*
1	Delay in Inpatient Registration	MRO	Duty RMO	CSA RMO	15 Minutes
2	Non-availability of Wheel-chairs and Stretchers	Staff Nurse/Head Nurse	Doctor (Assistant Professor)	Unit Chief (Professor / Associate Professor)	30 Minutes
3	Refusal for Admission	Assistant Professor	RMO	CS RMO (Pediatrics and OBGY)	1 Hour
4	Delay in Treatment by the Doctor	Staff Nurse/Head Nurse	Unit Chief (Professor /Associ-ate Professor)	Duty RMO	1 Hour
5	Doctor/Staff Not Available	Duty RMO	CS RMO (Pediatrics and OBGY)	Superintendent	30 minutes

6	Quality of Food	Staff Nurse/Head Nurse	Dietician	RMO Concerned	4 Hours
7	Beds and Linen	Staff Nurse/Head Nurse	Unit Chief (Professor /Associate Professor)	RMO concerned	1 Hour
8	Delay in Laboratory Reports	Staff Nurse/Head Nurse	Doctor (Assistant Professor)	Unit Chief and Chief of Lab concerned	1 Hour
9	Non-availability of Medicine	Staff Nurse/Head Nurse	Doctor (Assistant Professor)/ Pharmacist	Stores Medical Officer/ RMO	24 Hours
10	Cleanliness of Toilets and Bathrooms Inside Wards	Staff Nurse	Head Nurse	Unit Chief (Professor / Associate Professor)	30 Minutes
11	Cleanliness of Toilets and Bathrooms Outside	RMO concerned	CS RMO (Pediatrics and OBGY)	Superintendent	
12	General Cleanliness Outside the Wards	RMO Concerned	--	--	30 Minutes
13	Plumbing Problems	RMO Concerned	CS RMO (Pediatrics and OBGY)	Superintendent	1 Hour
14	Electrical Fittings	Staff Nurse/Head Nurse/Unit Chief	Electrician	RMO Concerned	1 Hour
15	Demanding of Bribes	Unit Head	RMO	CS RMO (Pediatrics and OBGY)	
16	Demanding of Bribes During Night Time	DSO/DMO	RMO/Duty RMO	CS RMO (Pediatrics and OBGY)	On completion of enquiry
17	Security Staff	RMO Concerned	CS RMO (Pediatrics and OBGY)	Superintendent	30 Minutes
18	Complaint against Staff Behaviour	RMO concerned	CS RMO (Pediatrics and OBGY)	Superintendent	1 Day

Outpatient Grievance Redressal Procedure

S. No.	*Nature of Grievance*	*Level One*	*Level Two*	*Time line*
1	Non-availability of Wheel-chairs and Stretchers			30 Minutes
2	Delay in Treatment by the Doctor			1 Hour
3	Doctor/Staff Not Available			30 minutes
4	Delay in Laboratory Reports			1 Hour
5	Non-availability of Medicine			24 Hours
6	Cleanliness of Toilets and Bathrooms			
7	Demanding of Bribes			
8	Security Staff			30 Minutes
9	Complaint against Staff Behaviour			1 Day

Note: DSO=Duty Surgical Officer
MRO=Medical Records Officer
DMO=Duty Medical Officer
RMO=Resident Medical Officer
CSA RMO= Civil Surgeon Assistant Resident Medical Officer

Grievance Redressal–List of concerned RMOs for Maintenance of Sanitation and Security Services–Ref. Rc.no. Peshi/GHS/2009, Date: 06.08.2009

S. No.	Name of the Doctor	Allocation of Responsibility Floor wise
1.	Dr. B.S. Prasad Rao, Dy. Civil Surge on RMO II	1st and 2nd floor (I.P Block)
2.	Dr. S. Prameela, C.A.S. RMO	3rd and 4th Floor (I.P. Block)
3.	Dr. B. Ranga Rao, CAS RMO	5th and 6th floor (I.P. Block)
4.	Dr. P. Chandra Sekhar Rao, CAS RMO	7th and 8th Floor (I.P. Block)
5.	Dr. T. Naresh Babu, CAS RMO	Complete out patient block (Casualty)

The following RMOs are entrusted with the duties of supervision of areas as mentioned against their names. Ref No.Peshi/GHS/2009 dt.26.08.2009

S. No.	*Name of the Doctor*	*Allocation of responsibility (floor-wise)*
1.	Dr. B. Venkateshwar Rao	All in all Sanitation (Total Hospital), H.D.S., Overall supervision of RMOs and C.M.Os (Posting, Duty Rosters), Paying Rooms, M.R.D. Linen, Computer Networking, Nodal Officer for KPI and Audit
2.	Dr. Vijaya Sree	Pediatrics and Obst. and Gynecology, Sanitation (Paed, Ob&Gy) Nursing Staff, Diet Canteen (Cleanliness and Quality of Food) Miscellaneous Stores.
3.	Dr. B.S. Prasad	Security Staff, Lifts, Class IV
4.	Dr. B. Ranga Rao	Parking, Ambulance, Central Suction, Oxygen Supply, Transport
5.	Dr. Prameela	O.P. Block, Hostels in O.P. Block, Duty Doctor Dinning Hall, Mess, Kitchen, Biomedical Waste, Mortuary
6.	Dr. Naresh Babu	VIP duties, Emergency Medicine Dept(Casualty), Indents, DMO/DSO Reports from Emergency Block, Bio Statistics, All Duty Rooms, Enquiry Room(Admission Room), EMRI-108
7.	Dr. P. Chandra Sekhar	Nursing School, Nursing Hostel, House Surgeons, Laboratory Services (Microbiology, Pathology, Biochemistry and Radiology)
8	Dr. Raana Reddy	Aarogyasri, Telephones, P.R.O., Media, Air conditioning, Civil Electrical, Plumber, Electrician Carpenter, Watermen.

Annexure 6.6

Patient's Guide Gandhi Hospital, Hyderabad

Welcome to the Gandhi Hospital

Gandhi Medical College and Hospital came into being on 14th September 1954. It has number of specialties. There are over 1000 beds and daily 1200 to 1500 patients are treated. As a patient of the hospital, your health and safety are our concern. Our doctors, nurses and other staff care for you to make your visit/stay in the hospital as comfortable as possible.

This patient guide gives you information about the Gandhi Hospital which will be of use to you. Please contact the Help Desk at the hospital if you require further information.

Hospital Services

The hospital has Inpatient, Outpatient and Emergency Services. The Outpatient registration timings are from 8.30 am to 11.30 a.m. New patients are seen by doctors up to 12 noon.

OP Departments:

1. General Medicine
2. General Surgery
3. Obstetrics and Gynecology
4. Pediatrics
5. Cardiology and Neurology
6. Gastroenterology
7. Venereology
8. TB & Chest Diseases
9. Psychiatry
10. Endocrinology
11. HIV Aids/VCTC
12. Dermatology
13. Nephrology
14. Psychiatry
15. Family Planning
16. Orthopaedics

Surgical Services:

1. Neuro Surgery
2. CT Surgery
3. Plastic Surgery, Burns
4. Urology
5. Ophthalmology
6. Dental
7. ENT
8. Pediatric Surgery

Other Facilities:

1. Radiological Laboratory
2. X-Ray, Ultra Sound
3. MRI CT Scan
4. Doppler, Colour Doppler
5. Mammography
6. IVP

Days of OP for Specialties:

S. No	*Description*	*Days of OP*
1	Urology	Monday, Tuesday
2	Neuro Physician	Tuesday, Thursday
3	Pediatric surgery	Monday
4	Endocrinology	Tuesday, Friday
5	Gastroenterology	Wednesday, Saturday
6	Cardiology	Wednesday, Saturday
7	Medicine	Every day
8	Orthopaedics	Every day
9	Gynaecology	Every day
10	Pediatrics	Every day

Inpatient and Emergency Services:

In- Patient and Emergency services are available 24 hrs round the clock. Intensive Care wards (IC) are available in IP and Emergency wards.

Contact "Enquiry Counter" at the Emergency ward or the "Help Desk" at the Outpatient Building.

Hospital Services are Free:

All services ion the Gandhi Hospital are rendered free of cost to the patients. If any person demands any money, please complain to the RMO/ Superintendent or to the Manager Help Desk in writing or by phone.

Payment Rooms:

Rooms are available for those who can pay fees for treatment. The fees and charges will depend upon the ward, illness and treatment, and investigative procedures. Details can be obtained from the Resident Medical Officer or at the Help Desk.

Help Desk and Patient Information Service:

A Help Desk is located at the Main Entrance of the Outpatient and Inpatient building for assisting the patients and visitors with information and to receive grievances.

The OP Help Desk works from 8:30 a.m. to 2:00 p.m. and Inpatient Help Desk works round the clock/24 hours

Patient Responsibilities:

As a patient you have the following responsibilities:

1. Keeping the premises clean.
2. Limiting the number of attendants to one.
3. Follow the advice of doctors and nurses.
4. Bring to the notice of head nurse, the presence of any un-authorized person in the ward.
5. Avoid wastage of water in bathrooms and toilets.
6. Don't throw food items outside the window, in wards, bathrooms and toilets. This will cause blockage to the drain.
7. All the treatment given in the hospital is free don't pay any money to anyone. In case of any such illegal demands please report to the Unit Head in the morning hours and Duty Medical Officer at nights.
8. Not to cause any nuisance or in-convenience to other patients in the ward.
9. Report all grievances in the form provided.
10. We will be happy to receive feedback from you on the services provided in the hospital at the time of discharge.

Diet/Breakfast & Meals for Inpatients:

Morning breakfast is served from 8.00 am to 8:30 a.m. Lunch is served from 1.00 pm to 2 p.m. and Dinner is served from 7.00 pm to 8.00 p.m. The Diet details are available with the Head Nurse and the patients can ask for these details from them.

If the patients have any complaints on the diet supplied they can register their grievance at the help desk, with the duty nurse or drop a complaint in the suggestion box.

Attendants Pass: Guidelines

- One attendant is allowed per patient.
- Security pass should be obtained by the attendants.
- The pass should be surrendered at the time of discharge of patient.
- The pass will be cancelled and pinned with the case sheet at the time of discharge.

Visiting Hours:

The visiting hours for the attendants are from 4.00 pm to 6.00 p.m. Infants and children are not allowed to visit patients in the hospital.

General Information: Health service volunteers to serve the needs of the patients are welcome to register at the Help Desk with details. Educational institutions wishing to offer social service in their curriculum are requested to contact the Hospital Superintendent.

Donations:

Donations are vital in maintaining the patient services. Donors may donate medical equipment, wheel chairs stretchers medicines or make a cash donation in the name of the Hospital Development Committee by Account paying cheques and obtain official receipt. Please contact the Hospital Superintendent in this regard.

Discharge from the Hospital:

As soon as the patient is ready for discharge, he/she will be informed. At the time of discharge, the patient will be given discharge summary report and test reports which should be safely preserved for future reference if required. Attendant pass issued at the time of admission of the patient should be surrendered before discharge.

Medical Records:

The Hospital preserves all Medical Records for a period of 10 years.

Ambulance:

Hospital Ambulance services are meant for referral cases. Private Ambulance services are available and can be hired. The details of available private Ambulance services can be obtained from the Help Desk.

Pharmacy:

A separate pharmacy for free supply of medicines is located:

- Outpatient building for outpatients
- In cellar of the inpatient building for the inpatients

In case the prescribed medicines are not available at the pharmacy, please lodge the complaint at the help desk giving particulars of the medicines not supplied.

Canteen:

Canteen services are available for attendance and visitors. The canteen is located at the cellar of the Inpatient building. Canteen is opened from 6.30 am to 9.00 pm on all days.

Valuables:

Get small amount of money along with you when you visit the hospital. Don't wear gold ornaments when you visit the hospital. Hospital Administration is not responsible for any loss of valuables of the patients during their visit in the Hospital.

Smoking:

Smoking is strictly prohibited in the Hospital. Chewing of *pan* and *gutka* and spitting are strictly prohibited. In case of violation a fine will be imposed as per the law.

Staff Identification:

All staff members have been given photo identity badges with their names and designation.

Grievances/Complaints:

For any grievances or complaints about our services please feel free to register your complaint at the Help Desk in the Outpatient/Inpatient wards, Staff Nurse or drop your complaints in the complaint box which have been placed at various points in the hospital.

Feed Back and Suggestions:

We welcome your feedback and suggestions. Please ask for the feedback form and fill it up to help us provide better services.

Suggestion boxes are placed at key locations in the Hospital for dropping your valuable suggestions. Please make use of the suggestion boxes.

Complaints and suggestions for feedback may also be communicated through the website of the hospital at *www.gmc.ap.nic.in*

Our Contact Phone Numbers/E-Mail/Website:

The general PBX Number is	–	27505566 (6 lines)
Hospital Superintendent	–	27505566
Direct No.	–	24505560
RMO and Administrator	–	23706732
Cell	–	9949095007
RMO II (Nodal Officer)	–	27555123, cell: 9866006611

Website	*www.gmc.ap.nic*
E-Mail	gandhihosp_hyd@yahoo.com

Telephone Numbers of Doctors in the Wards/Specialities can be obtained from the Help Desk.

7

Conclusion

The citizen's charters initiative in India started in 1997, with the Government of India (GoI) providing a direction for its implementation through comprehensive guidelines for charter implementation. During the past two decades of charter implementation by government departments at the centre and state, a new era in public administration and governance at large has been ushered in which is sensitised on issues of accountability, responsiveness, transparency and citizen centricity. Although the citizen's charter programme was launched by GoI and by many state governments with varied degrees of interest and focus, introduction of this new concept has not been very easy during the early stages of its implementation.

The old bureaucratic set-up and procedures as well as the rigid attitudes of the workforce in the government created a lot of initial hindrance in the implementation of citizen's charter. The formulation of citizen's charters in most of the cases has been an exercise that was carried out reluctantly because there was a direction from the top political bosses baring a few exceptions. We all know that in order to succeed in charter implementation, there is a need for commitment from the organisational top leaders, political bosses as well as civil servants, but the key for successful implementation lies with the staff who are at the cutting edge and at the public interface. Until and unless they appreciate the benefits of this scheme, it is practically impossible to see any results on the ground. To put it precisely, the employees who are responsible for its implementation must have proper sensitisation and orientation towards the citizen's charter process.

Involving cutting-edge staff and employees during the process of developing service standards is very critical. If cutting-edge staff are not involved in the development of standards and redress policies, they will not be ready to face the challenges of implementation. When organisations fail to deliver the quality of service that they have promised to customers and there are complaints regarding the service, the cutting-edge staff needs to be able to take decision immediately. Therefore, it is very important to empower front-line staff to make decisions. In most cases, this is not done in most of the organisations and there is a waiting period for decision making and cutting-edge staff wait for decisions to come from senior management.

It is very important that the employees should also be aware of the benefits and challenges of charter implementation and must be adequately prepared to face the citizens at the front end, because it is the front-end staff that bears the brunt during implementation of these kinds of initiatives.

Process re-engineering and streamlining systems are an integral part of the citizen's charter implementation process. Citizen's charters have succeeded in organisations which have attempted to refine their key processes so that they are able to deliver services promised to citizens on time. Clarity in roles and responsibilities of employees in the organisation and proper monitoring of performance are also essential for the success of charters.

One of the key elements of charter is grievance redressal system. The relevance of this system is that if the complaints received from citizens are actually worked upon and seriously understood the organisation will be able to tackle its major problems. The complaints received thus, can be used as a basic data on which problems can be identified and re-engineering process can be initiated. Citizen surveys, face-to-face contact with customers and different types of customer voice tools can be used for undertaking this activity. On the demand side, there are aspects like awareness campaigns to educate clients about the charter. Educating customers about the services is a very critical issue. It is observed that often services don't work unless customers come up and join hands with the service delivery organisations e.g., tax agencies can't send speedy refunds if taxpayers don't fill out their returns completely and accurately. Permit offices cannot process permits rapidly if developers hide information from them. In cases like these, the customer responsibilities are very important to keep up the service standards and guarantees.

In UK, citizen's charter implementation is reviewed on an annual basis and during these reviews it was found that the front-line employees who are responsible to deliver the standards in the charter are often well placed to offer practical suggestions for improvements, but unfortunately in most agencies these people are not consulted and recognised.

In the case of India, initially we had not done an annual review of charters but there have been evaluations carried out by reputed agencies across India to understand the implementation issues in charter implementation. During the various evaluations conducted by GoI, the need to involve citizens and staff to be consulted at every stage of formulation of the charter has come out strongly. Their orientation about the salient features and goals/objectives of the charter; vision and mission statement of the department, and handling of grievances and communication skills are very crucial. Need for wider publicity of the charter through print media, posters, banners, leaflets, handbills, brochures, local newspapers, etc., and also through electronic media came out very strongly in the review.

GoI introduced initiatives on citizen's charter implementation to all public service delivery agencies and also extended this initiative to banking sector as it has lot of customer interface. The advantage in the banking sector was that there was extensive use of IT (information technology) that banks had adopted to speed up various processes. The primary objective of the government was to build the banking sector as a model of excellence in the implementation of the citizen's charter. Three major national level banks, namely, Punjab National Bank, Punjab and Sind Bank, and Oriental Bank of Commerce, were selected for a hand-holding exercise by the Department of Administrative Reforms and Public Grievance (DARPG) in the year 2000. It was noted that these banks did exemplary implementation of the citizen's charter and there was complete stakeholder involvement in the formulation of citizen's charters. Charters were deployed in the banks by full involvement of the staff, specially the employees at the cutting-edge level and there was a lot of effort in creating awareness about the charter amongst the customers of the banks. Special training was given to all employees about the concept and implementation of citizen's charter. GoI also undertook an evaluation of the charters for the identified banks through independent agencies and action plans were chalked out to rectify shortcomings (Parigi and Geeta, 2002). The charters were, accordingly, revised and standardised on the basis of the model/mother charter developed by the Indian Banks Association (IBA). Training for employees of selected branches through master trainers, trained by the National Institute of Bank Management (NIBM) using a module developed in consultation with Department of Administrative Reforms and Public Grievances was organised.

The government continued its efforts all along to usher in transparency in the working of public service delivery agencies through multiple reform initiative. The recent step taken by the government is a commendable effort to integrate and sustain citizen's charter programme. In 2009, GoI established a Performance Management Division in the Cabinet Secretariat, headed by a secretary. Substantial marking has been allotted to the departments under the Results Framework Document (RFD) system followed by Government of India. An organisation is thus mandated to develop a Citizen/Client Charter as per the requirement of the current performance management system.

The Results Framework Document which is a mandatory requirement to be fulfilled by all government departments at the central level also includes citizen's charter implementation as one of the key criteria for assessment. The government realises that even if the charters and grievance redressal mechanisms (GRMs) are well drafted and the process of developing them is *sevottam* compliant, there is no guarantee that they will be implemented effectively. To ensure that they are implemented effectively, each ministry/department is mandated to determine beforehand the criteria and methodology by which they will be evaluated (Cabinet Secretariat, 2011).

As per the guidelines issued by the government, under the charter implementation the departments are mandated to design citizen's charter identifying various services to be delivered specifying timelines of delivery. They also have to design a grievance redressal system with specified timelines for redress and mechanism for appeal in case the grievances are not redressed on time and assign appropriate weightages to each service standard including timelines for redress of grievances.

Making citizen's charter an integral component of the performance management system has been a major step in the process of ensuring sustainability and continuity in the process of service delivery improvements. The Citizens' Charter experiment in India can be further strengthened if each government department/organisation can contribute to this initiative and strengthen citizen governance by identifying services to be provided by each of them and specifying timelines for efficient service delivery and evaluate themselves against these set standards. These initiatives will satisfy the general public and create a general sense of satisfaction. The departments/organisations must also focus on creating a robust framework to ensure the progress from formulation of charters to implementation of charters, from implementation to receiving citizen feedback and from citizen feedback to review, evaluation and updating of charters. This complete loop will bring in citizen satisfaction and establish good governance in the country. In building such a framework, the critical areas that have a bearing on the efficient and effective service delivery to the citizens through the charters need to be continuously monitored leading to corrective and timely steps to ensure their success. The implementation of citizen's charter is an ongoing exercise because it has to reflect the extensive and continual changes taking place in the domain of public services. Indian Government continuously strives to serve the citizens in an effective and efficient way so as not only to meet but to exceed their expectations. The citizen's charter initiative is a major step in this direction.

There are a number of lessons learnt and varied examples available nationally and internationally with the charter implementation process. The citizen's charter experience can be summed up as follows:

- Key to success of citizen's charter implementation is complete government support from the top leadership to the implementation of the programme.

- Preparing the organisation for implementing charters is very critical and it has been observed that the organisation that have prepared a base within the organisation for this change have been successful in implementation.
- Preparation also involves training and capacity building of the staff and personnel who are involved in the implementation of the charters.
- Extensive consultations with the key stakeholders are a key factor for the successful implementation of the charters.
- Accessibility of concerned officers in the organisations for assistance in case of any problem encountered by the citizen.
- Developing Service Delivery Standards is one of the key elements for effective implementation of the charters.
- Display of charters is another important concern in the charter implementation.
- Internal review and monitoring of charters in most of the cases has given the required impetus to successful implementation.
- Feedback from end users in regular intervals as a method of internal corrections has proved very useful.
- Awareness generation among public about the existence of the citizen's charters is a key factor in the charter implementation scheme.

Citizen's charters should be seen as:

- A partnership between people and the government.
- Citizen's charter is not a concept but a programme of action.
- They are a part of democratic reforms.
- Citizen's charters give people orientation and customer focus.
- Citizen's charters are a proactive approach to good governance.
- Political parties, administrators and even judiciary must encourage citizen's charters.

Table 7.1

Citizen's Charter: Trouble-Shooting Tips

Nature of Problem	*Cause*	*Solutions*
Limited awareness of the Charter among the public	• Absence of a planned approach to publicity • Limited training and stakeholder involvement • Charter treated as one among the many initiatives	• A holistic approach to publicity through press, electronic media and user involvement • Meet the citizen programmes by the departments
Poor or inadequate consultations with stakeholders and lack of citizen involvement throughout the charter cycle	• Bureaucratic style of functioning • No systematic identification of stakeholders • Lack of citizen friendly approach and absence of avenues for the stakeholders to interact or give feedback • Poor complaint redressal systems	• Change in the behaviour of the officers and staff through coaching, training and incentive systems • Creating customer friendly environment in the offices • Improved accessibility of officers and staff
Poor service delivery standards and under-performance	• Poor systems in place • Outdated processes • Staff not trained properly • Centralisation	• Training of staff at all levels • Decentralisation and delegation of authority • Technology upgradation • Process review and restructuring
Inadequate feedback from citizens about quality of service, limiting the impact of the charter	• Lack of transparency • Communication failure • Absence of systems to give feedback • Lack of credibility and lack of confidence in the system	• Customer confidence building measures sharing information and reports with users of the service • Consultation committees. Welcoming negative feedback and removing fear from customers. Assurance that information from feedback will be used to improve services.

Source: *A Guide to Developing and Implementing Citizen's Charter*, CGG, Hyderabad.

Some Tips to Make the Charters a Success

To make the citizen's charters a success, the following are needed:

- Organisation must develop a sense of urgency and identify the need for charter implementation.
- Owning of the charter by the head of the department and the entire staff.
- A committee headed by the top political bosses and civil servants to oversee the implementation and progress of the Citizen's Charters.
- Constant interaction with the stakeholders and users at large.
- Motivating the staff and performance review of the staff based on the criteria outlined in the charter.
- Accepting the need to change and taking corrective measures as and when required.
- Simplification of procedures and systems to bring in greater efficiency.
- Reducing hierarchy, decentralisation.
- Using technology appropriately.

In the present context, various state governments have implemented their Right to Public Service Acts and at the same time the GoI is implementing the Results Framework Documents (RFDs) with citizen's charter as a mandatory indicator. Departments/ministries may have to be very clear on how they are developing their charters and what they are promising because there are stringent measures of implementation of the programme by the government. This will also provide an opportunity for departments to assess their processes all over again and see how they can improve the same in order to reach acceptable levels of service delivery. Here are some suggestions:

- Proper identification of the services to be included as a part of the Citizen's Charters as well as services to be covered under the Right to Public Service Acts.
- Undertake strategic review of the department/ministries and make a thorough assessment of roles and responsibilities. Let

the employees know their jobs clearly and ensure no overlap of functions in the organisation.

- Use IT for making processes simpler and faster wherever possible.
- Establishing single window counters for providing services and giving of receipts with a timeline for the completion of a service go a long way in service delivery improvements.
- At the local levels and at service centres, the units must be properly staffed in order to cater to service delivery effectively.
- Monitoring from the top bosses is a must for enhancing efficiency of any organisation.
- Use customer feedbacks to identify issues and resolve them immediately. Using other grievance redress and accountability mechanisms such as public hearings by top level officials, grievance redress officers, auditors, and anti-corruption prosecutors also goes a long way in resolving matters.
- Check corrupt practices, identify these practices and processes and check them and nib them at the point of origin. Use IT and users wherever such practices appear to curb them.

References

Parigi, V.K. and P. Geeta (2002). *A Guide to Developing and Implementing Citizen's Charter*. Centre for Good Governance, Government of Andhra Pradesh.

Cabinet Secretariat (2011). *Guidelines for Designing and implementing Sevottam Compliant Citizen's Charter and Grievance Redressal Mechanism for Central Government Departments and Ministries* Performance Management Division, and Department of Administrative Reforms and Public Grievances, New Delhi.